The Science of Music

Other Books by Melvin Berger

Computers: A Question and Answer Book
Mind Control
Computers in Your Life
The New Earth Book: Our Changing Planet
The Supernatural: From ESP to UFOs
Enzymes in Action

SCIENTISTS AT WORK SERIES

Exploring the Mind and Brain
Sports Medicine
Disease Detectives
Police Lab

LET'S-READ-AND-FIND-OUT SCIENCE BOOKS®

Germs Make Me Sick!
Why I Cough, Sneeze, Shiver, Hiccup, & Yawn
Energy from the Sun
Switch On, Switch Off

Melvin Berger

THE SCIENCE
OF MUSIC

Illustrated by
Yvonne Buchanan

THOMAS Y. CROWELL   NEW YORK

The Science of Music

For information address Thomas Y. Crowell Junior Books,
10 East 53rd Street, New York, N.Y. 10022.
Typography by Andrew Rhodes

1 2 3 4 5 6 7 8 9 10

First Edition

Library of Congress Cataloging-in-Publication Data

Berger, Melvin.
   The science of music / by Melvin Berger :
illustrated by Yvonne Buchanan.—1st ed.
      p.   cm.
   Includes index.
   Summary: Discusses the physics of musical sound
and explains how the various musical instruments produce
sound, how records, tapes, and disks are made,
and how the playback equipment for them generates sound waves.
   ISBN 0-690-04645-6 : $
   ISBN 0-690-04647-2 (lib. bdg.) : $
   1. Music—Acoustics and physics—Juvenile literature.
2. Musical instruments—Juvenile literature.   3. Sound—
Recording and reproducing—Juvenile literature.   [1. Music—
Acoustics and physics.   2. Musical instruments.   3. Sound—
Recording and reproducing.]   I. Buchanan, Yvonne,
ill.   II. Title.
ML3928.B47 1988
781'.22—dc19
                                          87-24921
                                               CIP
                                           MN AC

Contents

1. The World of Sound   *1*
2. Sound and the Human Body   *16*
3. Strings   *28*
4. Percussion   *46*
5. Keyboards: Pianos, Organs, Synthesizers   *67*
6. Woodwinds   *84*
7. Brasses   *102*
8. Making a Record   *115*
9. Playback   *135*
   For Further Reading   *147*
   Index   *151*

The World of Sound

D o you know:
—what produces the sound when you blow
into a flute?
—why a trumpet's tone is different from that
of a violin?
—how recordings are made?
—how your stereo works?
—how electronic synthesizers imitate the sound of any instrument or voice?

In part, music is an art. Through the art of musical
composition, composers create music that communicates
their emotions and thoughts. Through the art of musical
performance, singers and instrumentalists turn the com-

poser's written notes into sound and express their own personalities in the process. Listeners hear the music and experience feelings and moods in response to the music.

At the same time, though, music is also a science. It is the science of how musical sounds are created and why there are high and low notes, loud and soft notes. The science of music also includes the study of how the human voice and all the various instruments produce their distinctive sounds, as well as how musical sounds are heard and how they are preserved and played back on records and tapes.

Making Sounds

All music is sound. And all sound is produced by vibration. Vibration is a very rapid shaking. Anything that vibrates produces a sound. Place your hand lightly on your throat as you sing or talk. Touch the side of a radio, stereo speaker, or television set as it is playing. Put a finger on a musical instrument while someone is playing it. Do you feel a trembling with your fingertips? You are feeling the actual vibrations that produce the sound of your voice, the radio, or the instrument.

When something is vibrating, the air surrounding it is also set vibrating. These vibrations spread out through the air as sound waves. The sound waves travel in all directions—up, down, and to every side.

Sound waves are invisible. But here is a way to picture what they look like. Place a wooden yardstick on a table with about half sticking out over the edge. Hold it down firmly on the table with the palm of your hand. Hit the far end of the yardstick; it starts to vibrate. Now imagine attaching a pencil to the end of the yardstick. Hit the yardstick again. As it vibrates up and down, think of pulling a piece of paper past the pencil point. The line drawn on the paper is similar to the invisible sound wave.

Although all sound is produced by vibration, all sounds

are not the same. There are soft sounds and loud sounds—a whisper is soft, a shout is loud. Sounds are also higher or lower in pitch—a flute plays high notes, a bass fiddle plays low notes. And sounds have different tone qualities—a piano has one tone quality, a guitar has another. That is why you can recognize the sounds of the different musical instruments.

Every musical sound can be identified by its loudness, pitch, and tone quality or tone color. Let's find out about the science of each of these aspects of sound.

Loudness

Everyone knows the difference between soft and loud sounds. But not everyone knows *why* the sounds differ. Here is a way for you to find out.

Place a wooden yardstick on a table as before. Hold it down firmly. Snap the end of the yardstick lightly to make it vibrate. Listen to the loudness of the buzz it makes and watch the vibration of the free end. Now hit the yardstick much harder. Again, listen to the sound and keep your eye on the end of the yardstick.

The second sound is louder than the first because you hit it harder and caused bigger vibrations. Loudness or softness is determined by the size of the vibrations. The bigger the vibrations, the louder the sound. The smaller the vibrations, the softer the sound.

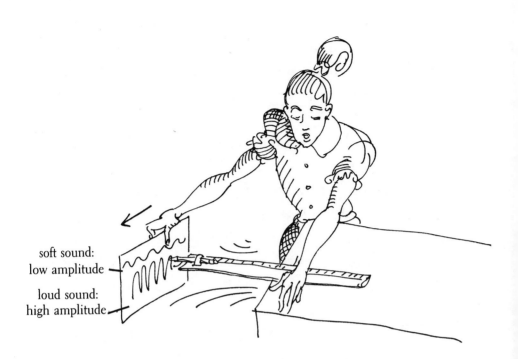

soft sound:
low amplitude

loud sound:
high amplitude

The back-and-forth distance that a vibrating object moves is called its amplitude of vibration. Imagine that you attach a pencil to the end of the yardstick and can see the vibrations on a strip of paper as you pull it past the pencil. For the soft sound the amplitude is quite small—the peaks are not very high, and the valleys are not very low. For the loud sound the amplitude is much bigger, with high peaks and low valleys.

The size of a vibrating body also affects the loudness of a sound. You can prove this yourself. Hold a fork and hit it on a table to make its prongs vibrate. Listen to the sound.

Now hit the fork again, but this time quickly hold the handle of the fork against the bare tabletop. The sound is louder because the fork is making the tabletop vibrate. The larger tabletop is able to set more air vibrating than the smaller fork.

Place a ticking watch or clock on a bare tabletop. Do you hear the ticking sounds get louder?

The loudness of a sound—its amplitude—is usually expressed in decibels. A decibel is one tenth of a bel, a unit named in honor of Alexander Graham Bell. The decibel is not a direct measurement. Rather, it is a ratio of loudness between any one sound and the softest sound that can be heard.

A sound that can just barely be heard is said to have a level of zero decibels. Every time the loudness doubles, the level jumps ten decibels.

Here are a few decibel ratings of familiar sounds:

rustling of leaves 10	noisy school cafeteria 80
whisper 20	moving train 100
average department store 60	jet engine 120
ordinary conversation 65	

Any sound over 120 decibels is felt as pain, rather than heard as sound. According to the U.S. government's Occupational Safety and Health Administration (OSHA), exposure for several hours to a sound level of over 92 decibels, such as at a loud rock concert, can cause permanent hearing damage.

Pitch

Sopranos sound different from baritones. Trumpets sound different from tubas. The notes on the right end of a piano keyboard sound different from those on the left end.

These sounds differ because they have different pitches. Some notes are high in pitch, others are low. Sopranos, trumpets, flutes, violins, and the right-hand notes of the piano are pitched high. Baritones, tubas, bassoons, bass fiddles, and the left-hand notes of the piano are low in pitch.

Pitch is determined by how fast something vibrates. The speed of vibration is known as frequency. The faster the vibrations, the higher the frequency and the higher the pitch. The slower the vibrations, the lower the frequency and the lower the pitch. Frequency is usually expressed as the number of times an object vibrates in a second.

A simple experiment with a yardstick can illustrate the basic principle of high and low pitch. Hold the yardstick with 9 inches on the table and 27 inches extending. Hit the free end. Listen to the sound and watch the end of the yardstick vibrate. Now slide it so that 18 inches are on the table and 18 inches extending. Hit it again.

Once more, listen and watch. Did the sound go up or down in pitch the second time? Did the vibrating end shake faster or slower? Because the part of the yardstick off the

high frequency:
high pitch
lower frequency:
lower pitch

table was shorter, it vibrated faster (had a higher frequency) and therefore had a higher pitch.

The line that would be made by a pencil attached to the vibrating end of the yardstick would show closely spaced peaks for the high-frequency, high-pitched note. For the low-frequency, low-pitched note, the peaks would be farther apart.

Humans can hear notes with frequencies from about 20 to 20,000 vibrations per second. Musical instruments, though, have a much narrower range. The lowest note of the piano has a frequency of just under 30 vibrations per second. The tuba goes down to only a little more than 40 vibrations per second. The piano's highest note vibrates over 4,000 times a second. The violin's top note has a frequency of about 3,500.

Tone Quality

Every instrument has its own individual, characteristic sound, which is known as its tone quality. The tone quality of a clarinet is not like that of a violin, trumpet, or piano. Even if all these instruments were playing the exact same note, you could tell them apart by their different tone qualities.

When you hear a tone played by a musical instrument, it sounds like a single pitch. Yet hidden within the sound are the sounds of several higher tones. These notes above the basic note are known as overtones. The overtones blend in so well with the sound of the basic note that you are usually not aware of them.

An interesting fact about the overtones is that they always vibrate two, three, four, five, etc., times as fast as the basic note. Put another way, the frequency of the overtones is always a whole number of times faster than the note that creates the overtone series. Thus, if the basic note vibrates 100 times per second, its overtones have frequencies of 200, 300, 400, 500, etc., vibrations per second.

Instruments have unique tone qualities because each one emphasizes different notes in the overtone series. The construction of the flute, for example, causes it to skip over the lower overtones and bring out the higher ones. The way the clarinet is built, on the other hand, causes it to stress the odd-numbered overtones. These differences make each instrument distinctive and unlike any other.

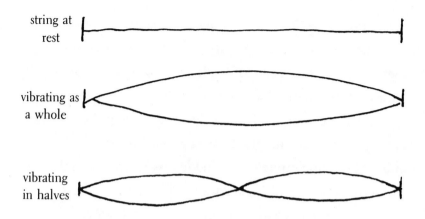

string at
rest

vibrating as
a whole

vibrating
in halves

Overtones occur because a vibrating body—such as a violin string, the column of air in a flute or trumpet, or the head of a drum—vibrates both in parts and as a whole. The vibrating of the entire violin string, for example, produces the basic note. But shorter lengths of the same string vibrate as well, producing the overtones. In the same way, the entire vibrating column of air in the wind instruments produces the basic note; shorter vibrating lengths produce the overtones. And the whole head of the drum produces the basic note, while the overtones come from the separate parts of the head vibrating.

Imagine tapping on a table with your whole hand at the rate of one tap per second. Now, at the same time, imagine tapping on the table with one finger at the rate of two taps a second. And, keeping the hand and one finger going, think of adding another finger tapping four times a second.

That is the way the musical instruments work. They vibrate (tap the table) at a basic speed. But at the same time their parts (fingers) are vibrating faster.

You can prove the existence of overtones on a piano. With your right hand press down the keys C, E, and G. Continue to hold the keys down after the notes have stopped sounding. The strings for these notes will be free to vibrate. Now hit a short, loud C two octaves lower with your left hand. Do you hear the higher notes faintly ringing, even though you did not play them? The notes C, E, and G are part of the overtone series for the note C. When you played the low C, it contained the overtones C, E, and G, which set the higher notes vibrating and caused them to sound.

Try this again. This time, however, press down three different notes—say B, D, and F. These notes are not in the C overtone series. Hit the lower C again. You do not hear any high ringing notes because B, D, and F are not part of the C overtone series.

Because each type of instrument emphasizes different overtones in the overtone series, the actual picture of a sound wave made by a particular instrument does not look much like the imaginary line you drew with the vibrating yardstick. There is the basic up-and-down wave movement of the line. But added to that are many extra rises and falls caused by the overtones. This produces sound waves that are very complex.

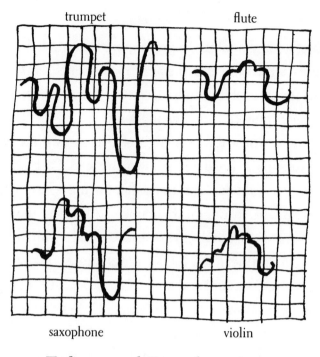

trumpet   flute

saxophone   violin

Echoes and Reverberations

As sound waves move out into the air, they bump into many different kinds of objects. Some are soft, like curtains and rugs, upholstered furniture, and clothing. When this happens, the waves are soaked up like water into a sponge. But sound waves also strike hard surfaces, like floors, walls, ceilings, and closed windows. When sound waves hit these surfaces, they bounce back like light rays reflected by a mirror.

Sound waves that bounce off a hard surface are heard twice—once when the sound is made and again when it is bounced back. A sound that takes one tenth of a second or longer to return is said to have an echo. Shout your name in a large gymnasium, or outdoors in a cave or canyon, or between tall buildings. The sound of your name that seems to call back to you is an echo.

If you shout your name in a tunnel or a tiled bathroom, though, the sound is different. The sound bounces back and forth repeatedly between the hard walls and becomes blurred. This overlapping of sound is known as reverberation.

A room that produces echoes or reverberations can be very uncomfortable. It is hard to follow any music that is being played, because the old sounds are still echoing as the new ones begin—the ear cannot sort them out. And it can be difficult to understand what people are saying for the same reason. One way to stop these annoying sounds is to place more soft furniture, drapes, or carpets in rooms that have too much reverberation. Another way is to cover the ceiling or walls with sound-absorbent tiles. Tiles with soft surfaces or with many tiny holes absorb sound waves and prevent them from being reflected back.

Resonance

When the sound of one vibrating object sets another object vibrating, this is known as resonance. The vibrations actually pass from object to object.

Resonance occurs when a nearby object has the same natural frequency (speed of vibration) as the object producing the sound. To hear the natural frequency of various objects, lightly tap different things around you with a pencil. It is especially easy to hear the natural frequencies of drinking glasses of various sizes and shapes. If a musician were to play a note with the same exact frequency as a certain glass, for instance, the glass would be set vibrating. The glass would be resonating. Other notes would make the glass vibrate, but with much less amplitude.

You have probably heard stories of singers able to shatter glasses with a single note. It can happen! If the vibrations of the singer's voice are at the exact frequency of the glass, if the glass is thin, and if the sound is loud enough, the glass will crack.

You can use a piano to create your own resonance. Press down the right-hand pedal. This allows all the strings to vibrate. With the lid of the piano raised, aim your voice at the piano strings and loudly sing any note. Listen carefully and you will hear resonance from the string tuned to the frequency of the note you sang. Sing other notes into the piano. With each note you should hear the resonance from the piano string with the same frequency. You will also hear other strings vibrating, more faintly, in resonance with the overtones in your voice.

Some objects are able to vibrate or resonate at any pitch. Loudspeakers and the bodies of most musical instruments will resonate for a wide range of frequencies. For example, if you hold your fingertips on the body of a guitar or violin while loud music is being played in the same room, you will feel the instrument resonating for all the sounds.

A seashell vibrates in the same way. You may think that when you hold a large seashell to your ear, you are hearing the roar of the ocean. Actually, the shell is resonating to all the sounds around you, including many that you are not even aware of. The curved walls of the shell cavity reflect these sounds back and forth so that they sound like ocean waves.

We live in a world full of wonderful sounds. We go to concerts, operas, and other musical events. We hear music on records and tapes, radio and TV. We hear background music in offices, factories, and stores. Many of us make music ourselves. All this leads us to ask the question: How does the science of sound join with the art of music to create the glorious sounds we hear?

Sound and the Human Body

All sound, we said, is vibration. The vibrations of the sound producer make the surrounding air vibrate. And these vibrations travel out through the air. Some of these vibrations reach people's ears and those people hear the sounds.

But exactly *how* do people hear sound?

The Ear and Hearing

Our ears consist of three sections—the outer ear, middle ear, and inner ear.

The cuplike shape of the outer ear, or auricle, collects the sound waves passing through the air. From here the

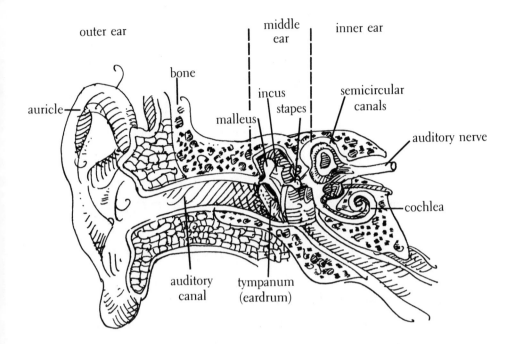

outer ear

middle ear

inner ear

bone

auricle

malleus

incus

stapes

semicircular canals

auditory nerve

cochlea

auditory canal

tympanum (eardrum)

vibrations pass through the one-and-a-half-inch-long auditory canal to the middle ear.

At the inner end of the auditory canal, where the middle ear begins, the vibrating sound waves strike against the eardrum, or tympanum. This is a thin, flexible membrane a quarter inch across. It is stretched like a tight drumhead across the inner end of the auditory canal. Sound waves set the eardrum vibrating at the same frequency as the sound waves themselves.

Behind the eardrum are three tiny movable bones. These are the hammer (malleus), anvil (incus), and stirrup (stapes). The hammer, which looks like a miniature carpenter's hammer, is attached to the eardrum. When the eardrum vibrates, the hammer vibrates too. The vibrating hammer beats against the tiny anvil, which resembles the anvil that blacksmiths use. The anvil, in turn, is made to vibrate. The vibrating anvil fits into the stirrup, which is shaped like the ones on a horse's saddle. The stirrup in turn picks up the vibrations. And the stirrup passes the vibrations to the oval window of the inner ear, called the labyrinth.

The main part of the inner ear is the cochlea. The cochlea is a liquid-filled tube, one and a half inches long, that is curved in a spiral like a snail's shell. Nerve endings in the cochlea sense the pattern of the vibrations and change them into a pattern of tiny impulses of electricity. These electrical signals travel through the auditory nerve to the brain, where the sound is given meaning.

In a way, the ear works like a telephone. When you speak into a telephone, the sound waves are changed into electrical impulses. The impulses then travel through wires to the other phone, where they are changed back into sound. Likewise, sound waves that reach your ear are changed into electrical nerve impulses. These impulses flash through certain nerves to the brain, where they are perceived as sound and the sound is given a meaning.

The Voice

Whether it is used for everyday talking or for singing an operatic aria, for shouting or for whispering, the human voice is an amazing sound producer. It involves the throat, mouth, nose, and chest to produce its remarkable range of sounds.

The sound of your voice begins in your throat. The throat contains two passages. At the front is the windpipe, or trachea, which goes to the lungs. Behind is the food pipe, or esophagus, which leads to the stomach. When you breathe, the air goes to the windpipe. When you eat, the food is sent to the food pipe.

Inside the windpipe is a stiff structure, the larynx. The larynx is made of cartilage, the same material that supports your outer ear and nose. If you rub your hand lightly up and down the front of your throat you can feel a bump. People often call it the Adam's apple. The Adam's apple is the front point of your larynx. When you swallow, you can feel your Adam's apple and larynx move up and down.

Stretched from front to back across the larynx are two bands of elastic tissue called the vocal cords. It is the vocal cords that vibrate to make the sounds we speak or sing. If you hold your hand lightly against your Adam's apple when you use your voice, you can feel the vibrations of your vocal cords and larynx.

Most of the time, the two vocal cords are relaxed and

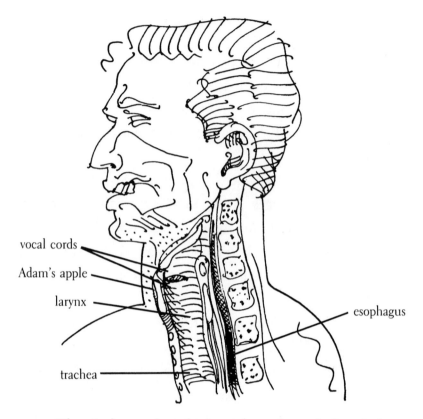

vocal cords

Adam's apple

larynx

esophagus

trachea

apart. The air that we breathe in and out through the windpipe passes easily between them without causing any vibrations. There is, therefore, no sound.

When we want to talk or sing, though, we automatically tighten the muscles in the larynx. This pulls the vocal cords together. The passage between them becomes very narrow. The air passing between them sets the vocal cords vibrating, and sound is produced.

As children get older, their vocal cords grow longer. Around age twelve, boys' vocal cords suddenly start to grow much heavier and longer. While a boy's vocal cords are growing, the muscles of his larynx have difficulty learning to move these larger cords. As the muscles are getting used to their new job, the boy's voice jumps up or swoops down, and is beyond his control. We say the boy's voice is cracking. By age fifteen this period of rapid growth is usually over. The vocal cords are now about two thirds of an inch long. Men's voices are lower in pitch than those of girls or women, whose vocal cords are about half an inch in length.

Curiously enough, a man's body size has nothing to do with the length of his vocal cords. Some short, thin men have long vocal cords and therefore low-pitched voices. And there are tall, big men with short vocal cords and high-pitched voices. Men whose vocal cords are long and thick and vibrate at slower speeds sing down low and are called basses. Other men with shorter, thinner vocal cords sing a higher range of notes and are called tenors.

The vocal cords of women seldom get as long as men's. Women with the shortest cords sing highest of all. They are called sopranos. Those with slightly longer cords sing lower and are the altos.

For you to sing different pitches, the muscles in your larynx must change the tightness of your vocal cords. Hold your fingers lightly against the front of your throat and sing a very low note. Now switch to a very high note. Did you feel your larynx jump up as you switched pitch? The movement was caused by the muscles tightening the vocal cords to produce the high note.

Let's see how tightness affects pitch. Blow up a balloon. Hold the lip of the balloon with the forefingers and thumbs of both hands. Listen to the sound of the air rushing out as it sets the lip of the balloon vibrating. Now tighten the lip of the balloon by pulling your hands apart as you hold the lip pinched. Do you hear the air making a higher sound? Because the lip of the balloon is tighter, the vibrations are faster and the pitch is higher.

The sounds produced by the vibrations of your vocal cords are not very loud. To be heard at any distance, they need to be built up, or amplified. This is done by adding resonance to the original sound with your chest, throat, nose, and mouth.

Your chest acts as a resonator when you sing low notes. Hold your hand on your chest and loudly sing the deepest notes you can. You'll feel your chest vibrating and adding resonance to the sound. Have you ever read about gorillas beating on their chests to frighten an enemy? The resonance created by the ape's chest produces a sound like that of a booming drum.

Your throat adds resonance to notes of all pitches, high and low. Hold your hands on both sides of your throat as you sing notes of different pitches. Do you feel the vibrations?

Your nose, also, is a resonator for all notes. Pinch your

nostrils closed with two fingers and sing up and down the scale on the word "me." You will feel that the vibrations are passed to your nose as well.

Do you know that you actually change the shape of your mouth to resonate at different pitches? Form your mouth to say "ah," but don't actually say it. Tap your front teeth lightly with a pencil. You'll hear a low tone. Next form your mouth to say "ee" and tap again. This time you'll hear a higher tone. In both cases the mouth added resonance to the soft tap of the pencil.

Try this out. Cup your hands slightly and clap them together just in front of your mouth so that they drive air into your mouth. As you continue clapping your hands, open your mouth wide for "ah." Then gradually close it for "ee." You'll hear the pitch rise as you go from one mouth shape to the other.

Without using your vocal cords, breathe your name. You can hear it very softly. But if you hold your ears, you will hear it quite clearly. A person who has laryngitis and cannot use his or her vocal cords will very often breathe out words, or whisper. As the breath passes through the mouth, it is set vibrating. Since the mouth can tune to so many different pitches, we are able to produce whispered speech.

There are, therefore, two aspects to using the human voice: The vocal cords must be made to vibrate at the right pitch, and the resonators—the chest, throat, nose, and mouth—must add loudness to the sound.

Voice Quality

Can you immediately recognize the sound of your friend's voice? Most people can. The reason is that everyone has a unique voice, just as everyone has his or her own fingerprints.

Why?

No two people have exactly the same size vocal cords. Nor do they have the same size and shape chest, throat, nose, and mouth. These various combinations create different overtones for the sounds that every person produces. Overtones, you recall, are higher notes that blend in whenever a note is sounded. The quality of a person's voice is determined by which overtones are stronger and which are weaker.

You can prove this with the use of a piano. Open the piano lid. Press the right-hand pedal so that all the strings are free to vibrate. In a loud, clear voice say the names of the letters A, E, I, O, U, with your mouth close to the strings of the piano. You'll hear a ringing sound coming from the piano. It is caused by the vibrations of your voice setting the piano strings vibrating by resonance.

Listen carefully to the resonance your voice calls forth. Then ask a friend to say the same letters into the piano. Again the piano will begin to sound. But close listening will show that the sound is slightly different from yours. The reason is that the overtones in your friend's voice are not the same as the overtones in your voice. In general, since overtones are above the basic note, a higher-pitched voice causes higher sounds to ring from the piano. A lower-pitched voice produces both low and high piano notes.

The sounds of speech are divided into vowels and consonants. The vowels are A, E, I, O, and U, as well as W and Y. All the other letters are consonants. How are these different sounds produced by the human voice?

Take a deep breath. Close your lips tightly. Now open your lips suddenly, without using the voice. A puff of air pops out, and you hear the sound of the letter P. Do the same thing again, but this time use your voice—which means your vocal cords vibrate—as you open your lips. This produces the sound of the letter B. Both P and B are consonant sounds. All consonants are produced by blocking the breath, then exploding or squeezing it in some part of the mouth or throat. Pronounce some of the other consonants, and find out how and where you make them.

A vowel sound is a breath with sound, produced with no blocking. Each vowel sound has its own general pitch range. One way we control the pitch is by changing the position of the tongue in the mouth. Moving the tongue can make the vibrating column of air coming from the vocal cords narrower or wider. A narrow vibrating air column produces a higher pitch. A broad vibrating air column produces a lower pitch.

The highest-pitched vowel sound in English is the sound of E in "me." The tongue is arched up and forward to pronounce this E sound. The "oo" sound, as in "food," is our lowest-pitched vowel. It is pronounced with the back of the tongue arched and the lips rounded. Try saying the other vowels, paying particular attention to the position of the tongue and the shape of the mouth and lips.

There are a few important differences between speaking and singing. In singing the vowel sounds are held or extended longer. The singer's breath has to last for a longer time than for ordinary speech. We normally breathe about once every four seconds when we speak, but singers take breaths much less frequently. Singers use definite pitches and produce notes throughout a wide range. Speech is often not clear in pitch and does not go very high or low.

Sometimes people sing above their natural voice range. This is called falsetto. It is believed that falsetto singing uses just the edges of the vocal cords. A falsetto voice always sounds very thin and lacks tone color. Many pop singers use falsetto to sing above their normal range and for special effects. Some of the falsetto singing we hear today is of the type called yodeling. The mountain people of Switzerland are famous for their outstanding yodeling. American cowboy songs sometimes use yodeling also. Yodeling is a mixture of normal and falsetto tones, going back and forth rapidly from one to the other.

A few factors determine the loudness of the voice. One

is the size of the various resonators and how well the person uses them. More important, though, is the pressure with which the air is forced past the vocal cords. The stronger the air pressure, the louder the sound. Loudness also tends to vary with pitch. The vocal cords are tighter for the higher notes; therefore more air is needed to set them vibrating, and higher notes in speech or song usually sound somewhat louder than the rest.

To improve your voice, for both speaking and singing, you should breathe deeply and fill your lungs with air. Let your air flow out smoothly and strongly as you speak or sing. Take time to breathe in again. Use your tongue and mouth actively to form the right sounds. And avoid straining your voice by shouting or screaming. If you treat your vocal cords like the fine, delicate musical instrument that they really are, you will be rewarded with a richer, fuller-sounding speaking and singing voice.

Strings

The first string instrument probably dates back to prehistoric times. Many experts believe that it started as the bow of an ancient hunter's bow and arrow. The twang of the bowstring as it sent an arrow at the target must have been a pleasant and welcome sound. And the way the sound continued after the arrow was shot surely made the hunter feel good.

In time, people began to pluck bowstrings just to hear the pretty noises that they made. Gradually, over thousands of years, the hunter's bow was transformed into a musical instrument. Strings of different lengths and thicknesses were added to make it possible to play different notes. The strings were stretched over all sorts of boards and boxes to make

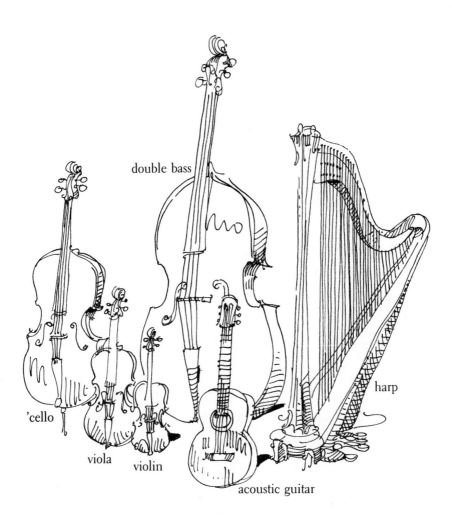

double bass

'cello

viola

violin

acoustic guitar

harp

their sounds louder and more attractive. And new ways were found to set the strings vibrating.

The story of the modern family of string instruments— harp, violin, viola, 'cello, double bass, guitar, and their relatives—that emerged from these humble beginnings is remarkable indeed.

· 29 ·

The Harp

The harp is the oldest member of the string family. Remains of harps have been found in Egyptian tombs that are 6000 years old! Modern harps are still made in the same basic shape as these ancient instruments. But while the old harps had no more than twenty-three strings, today's harps have forty-seven.

The most common harp is a large, triangular-shaped instrument that rests on the floor and is held between the knees of the seated player. The harp is played by plucking the strings, one at a time or several at once. An important member of most symphony orchestras, the harp can also be heard in solo concerts.

The strings on a modern harp vary in length from less than 3 inches to over 5 feet. The pitch that a string will produce is determined, in part, by its length—the shorter the string, the higher the pitch; the longer the string, the lower the pitch. The 3-inch-minus string, therefore, produces the harp's highest note, while the 5-foot-plus string sounds the lowest note on the instrument.

You can test this principle of sound production in a simple experiment. Stretch a rubber band around an empty, open cigar box or shoe box. Pluck the section of the rubber band that runs across the open top of the box and listen to the note it makes. Now, with two fingers of the other hand, pinch the same section of the rubber band near one end.

Hold the rubber band tightly where you are pinching, but do not pull it out of shape. Then pluck the rubber band again. Does the second note sound higher or lower than the first?

The note sounds higher because pinching the rubber band shortens its vibrating length. The band cannot vibrate beyond the point where you are holding it. And the shorter the string, the higher the pitch.

Try pinching the rubber band closer to the center and

pluck again. Do you hear the pitch go up even higher? It is possible to play a scale or a simple melody by pinching the rubber band at different points.

If you pinch the rubber band exactly in the middle, dividing it in half, the frequency doubles. The pitch then goes up eight notes, or an octave. Different octaves of the same note have the same letter name. As an example, the notes with frequencies of 110, 220, 440, and 880 are all different octaves of the note A.

The basic pitch of the harp string depends on its length. The pitch is also affected by the tightness of the string. The tighter any string is, the higher its pitch; the looser the same string, the lower its pitch.

If you arrive early at a concert, you may see the harpist on the stage tuning the instrument by adjusting the tightness of each string. The player changes pitch by turning the tuning pins to which the strings are attached. If a string is below the standard pitch, the harpist tightens the string by winding more of it onto the tuning pin. If a string is above the standard pitch, the harpist turns the pin the other way to loosen that string.

Often, though, harpists must change the pitch while they are playing. They do this by means of foot pedals. Before the first rehearsal the harpist looks over the music and plans how to use the harp's seven foot pedals, one for each note of the scale. The pedals change the pitch of the harp strings by changing their vibrating length.

Each pedal controls all the octaves of a particular note—one controls all the Cs, one all the Bs, and so on. When the pedal is in the top position, all the notes with that pitch name sound the *flat* of the original pitch: C flat, B flat, and so on. When the harpist moves the pedal to the middle notch, the mechanism shortens the vibrating length of those strings. All octaves of that note go higher; they go up a half step, to the natural note—C natural, B natural, etc. If the harpist pushes the pedal to the lowest notch, the string

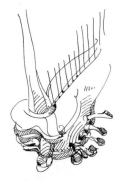

length is further shortened. All octaves of that note move up even higher; they have moved up a whole step from the original tuning, to the *sharp* of that note—C sharp, B sharp, etc. In this way, all possible notes are covered, and the player can play A flat, A natural, or A sharp. In fact, it is even possible to play the same exact note on two different strings—A sharp and B flat, say—which can be very helpful in fast, complicated music. Most harpists try to plan their pedal changes in advance, since it is almost impossible to move a pedal in the middle of a rapid passage.

· 33 ·

You can use the box and rubber band to prove that a tighter string gives a higher pitch. Pluck the rubber band as before and remember the note you heard. Now grasp the rubber band on the outside of the box and pull it down and away from the box. Make sure, though, that the rubber band is still resting solidly on both sides of the box. Since it is resting on the sides of the box, the vibrating length stays the same. All that you have changed is the tightness of the rubber band by stretching it out. Pluck the rubber band again. Do you hear the higher pitch? By tightening the rubber band, you raised the pitch.

In addition to length and tightness, thickness also helps to determine the pitch of the harp strings. Take a close look

at a harp. You'll notice that the strings are of different thicknesses, or diameters. The longer strings are much thicker than the shorter ones. The extra thickness makes these strings even lower in pitch. The shorter strings are thinner and are therefore pitched even higher.

With a few more rubber bands and the same box you can find out how pitch is affected by thickness. Collect some rubber bands of the same length but of different thickness. Put these rubber bands around the box so that the "playing" length and tightness are the same. Only their thickness varies. Pluck each one. Do you hear the thin ones ring higher in pitch than the thick ones?

The Violin Family

The string section of an orchestra is made up of four instruments that are related to the harp, yet are very different. The instruments are the violin, viola, 'cello, and double bass. (We write 'cello because the full name is violoncello, which is usually shortened.) Although they differ considerably in size and in range of pitches, these instruments are often grouped together and called the violin family.

Basically, each member of the violin family has four strings that are stretched across a wooden box. The instruments are played with a bow. Scraping the strings with the bow sets them vibrating. The vibrating string by itself would not create a very loud sound. But it rests on the bridge, an upright piece of light-colored wood on top of the violin's box. As the string vibrates, it sets the bridge vibrating. The design carved into the bridge allows the wood to shake back and forth freely.

The bridge, in turn, carries the vibrations to the top, or belly, of the violin—the surface of the box under the strings. The belly is made of a soft wood, such as spruce. A thin wooden post hidden inside the violin, called the sound post, transfers the vibrations from the belly to the back of the instrument. The back is made of a hard wood, such as curly maple. Since the belly and back of the violin are so much bigger than the bridge, they make even more air vibrate and thus amplify the sound.

But even the vibrating wood of the violin does not make a very big sound. The sound grows because the wood makes the air inside the instrument vibrate. The special shape of

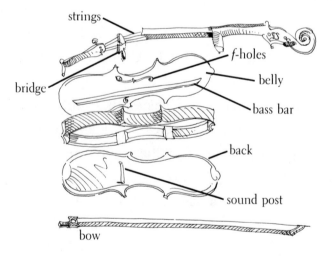

the violin body reflects the sound waves back and forth, making them stronger and much, much louder. It is like standing in a room lined with mirrors. You see yourself many times over. In the same way, the body of the violin bounces the sound around, giving it enough volume to fill the biggest concert hall. The sound comes out through the two so-called *f*-holes cut in the belly of the instrument.

To hear how reflection amplifies sound, you'll again need your rubber band and box. Pluck the rubber band in the same way as before and remember how loud it sounded. Now slide your thumb and index finger inside the box beneath the rubber band and lift the rubber band up away from the box. Holding the rubber band up with two fingers, pluck it again, just as hard as before. Notice how the sound is softer now, with the rubber band up in the air. The sound was louder when the rubber band was resting against the box. That is because the sound waves were reflected back and forth within the box and made louder.

Strings for the modern violin family, as well as harp strings, are made of metal, nylon, or gut. At one time, all strings were said to have been made of catgut. But it was later found that the catgut story was a lie told by some early string makers to confuse their competitors. The gut used is actually made from sheep intestines. The threads are treated chemically and woven into strands of great strength. On a violin, the individual strings are under a pull of around 70 pounds!

Have you ever wondered how the violin, with only four strings, can play along with the harp, which has forty-seven? Actually, you already know enough about the science of sound to figure out the answer!

All four strings are the same length. The four strings, though, are not of the same thickness. The first two, on the left as the violin is played, are heavier and thicker. They are made with a core that is covered with a tight winding of very thin metal wire that adds thickness and bulk. The third one is thinner; and the fourth string is thinnest of all.

Do you recall that thicker strings produce lower pitches? Even though the vibrating length of all four strings is the same, the thickness makes some strings sound lower. Those on the right, being thinner, are higher in pitch.

Besides being thicker or thinner, the strings are also tighter or looser. String players control the tightness of each string by means of the peg to which it is attached. Like harpists, string players tune their instruments before playing by turning the pegs. If the pegs have slipped or heat has caused the strings to expand, they tighten them. If the strings are cold and contracted, they loosen them.

Using the strings alone, players could play only four notes on the instruments of the violin family. Clearly, a way is needed to add more pitches. The basic method involves changing the length—or rather the vibrating length—of the strings. Players shorten the strings by pressing on them, at various points, with the fingers of the left hand. The fingers prevent the strings from vibrating past the contact point, thereby cutting the vibrating length. As you know, the shorter the vibrating length, the higher the pitch.

By using the fingers of the left hand (except the thumb) on all the strings, players are able to produce many different notes. With the left hand near the pegbox, the player can play the lowest notes on each string. But if the music is in a higher range, the player's hand moves toward the bridge to create shorter vibrating lengths.

The wooden part of the bow, with which the player sets the strings vibrating, is usually made of *pernambuco* wood from Brazil. This stick is both strong and flexible. Stretched over it are 200 hairs from a horse's tail. Each hair is rough and uneven. As the player scrapes the bow over the string, the friction of each strand grabs–releases, grabs–releases, grabs–releases, the string. The fact that all 200 hairs are pulling at the string at once gives a smooth, continuous sound.

To help the bow hairs tug at the strings, the string player rubs them with rosin before playing. Rosin, a by-product in the manufacture of turpentine, comes in a solid, glass-like cake. When rubbed on the bow hairs it comes off as a thick white powder. The rosin powder makes the bow hairs sticky and helps them set the strings vibrating.

Besides using the bow to produce the sound, string players can pluck the strings with the fingers of the right hand. This is known as playing *pizzicato*. It produces the same effect as plucking the strings of a harp. The notes are short and abrupt, compared to the long notes that can be produced with the bow.

The Viola, 'Cello, and Double Bass

The viola is similar to the violin in size and in the way it is held under the chin. The main difference is that it is larger. The viola is about 27 inches long, compared to the violin's 24 inches. The longer strings, which are also thicker, make the pitch lower. Actually, the viola's dark, rich tone is tuned four notes lower than that of the violin. Also, since it takes more energy to set the viola strings vibrating, the bow used to play the instrument is also slightly longer and heavier.

The 'cello is about 55 inches in length, just about twice as long as the viola. This makes the 'cello strings sound much lower in pitch and deeper in tone than the two smaller instruments. The 'cello's four strings are each seven notes (an octave) lower in pitch than the same strings on the viola. Cellists always sit when they play, holding the 'cello upright between their knees. They support it, though, on a thin metal rod at the bottom called the end pin. Violinists and violists may sit if they are playing as part of a group, but when playing solos they generally stand.

The biggest of the string instruments is the double bass— 6 feet 3 inches tall. This large instrument—also called bass or bass fiddle—stands vertically on a short wooden or metal end pin. Because of its size, double-bass players must stand or half sit on tall stools. Its great string length makes the double bass the lowest of the string instruments. Its bottom string is six notes lower than the 'cello's bottom string.

String Instruments: $100 to $1,000,000

To the untrained eye, any two violins, violas, 'cellos, or double basses look alike. They're the same size and shape, they're made from the same types of woods, and they use the same strings. Yet a cheap but playable string instrument can be bought for a hundred dollars or so. And an instrument by a great maker, such as Antonio Stradivari (Stradivarius) (1644–1737) or Giuseppe Guarneri (Guarnerius) (1698–1744), costs over one million dollars! Why this immense difference in price?

The simple answer is that the expensive string instruments

sound much, much better and are easier to play. Because the better instrument vibrates evenly throughout its range, its notes have a more consistent volume and tone quality. Also, fine instruments respond more quickly to the touch. As soon as the player pulls the bow across a string, a clear, beautiful note rings out. Cheaper instruments, on the other hand, are made from parts that are imperfectly matched. As a result, when a note is played on these instruments, there is a delay of a tiny fraction of a second before they "speak."

Players, and listeners too, can usually recognize the sound quality of a fine violin, viola, 'cello, or double bass. For a while it was thought that the varnish with which Stradivarius covered his instruments was the "secret ingredient." By now, though, his varnish has been chemically analyzed. It has been exactly duplicated and put on instruments—with no great improvement in sound. Another theory held that because the sap in the wood of the "old master" instruments had completely dried up over the 200 years since they were made, the wood could vibrate more freely. But sad to say, not all old instruments sound good.

One current idea is that Stradivarius and the other great makers had a special artistic approach to their craft. They were able to produce the ideal size and shape of their instruments more by touch and feel than by measurement. But even though modern makers can exactly duplicate the dimensions of the "old master" instruments, they seldom duplicate their sound quality.

In any case, the finest string instruments are limited in number and greatly prized. For example, of the 1200 instruments made by Stradivarius, only about 540 violins, 12 violas, and 50 'cellos survive. These superb string instruments set a standard against which all other instruments are judged today.

Guitars, Acoustic and Electric

The acoustic guitar has the same basic shape as the members of the violin family—but with some important differences. The top and bottom of the guitar are flat, while the belly and back of the violin bulge out. The guitar's box is wider and more than a foot longer than the violin's. In addition, most guitars have a low, flat bridge and six strings, not four. And the guitar sound comes out of a round opening near the center of the instrument, instead of two f-holes as in the violin.

The guitar is never bowed. The strings are plucked with fingertips or fingernails, or with a thin piece of plastic or metal called a pick or plectrum. The player can sound a single note, or several notes at once, or can strum by pulling quickly across several strings.

The science of the acoustic guitar is the same as that of the violin. The player plucks the string to set it vibrating. The bridge transmits the vibrations to the body, which amplifies the sound. The loudness is further increased by the reflection of the sound waves within the guitar body.

The basic pitches of the six guitar strings are determined by their tension and thickness. The players create all the other notes by changing the vibrating length of the strings. They do this by pressing the strings down onto raised metal bars, called frets, which stop the vibrations at the point of pressure.

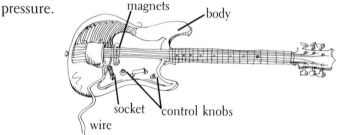

The electric guitar is similar to the acoustic guitar. But there are a few important differences. Instead of a hollow body, the body of the electric guitar is usually a solid piece of hard, heavy wood. Without the boost to the sound that a hollow body provides, the sound of a plucked string on the electric guitar is very soft and thin. The electric guitar, however, has built-in electric circuits that make the sound of the instrument as loud as the player wants.

The job of boosting the sound of the electric guitar starts with a small flat device called a pick-up, which is attached to the belly of the instrument. The pick-up is placed just under the guitar strings. It contains six tiny upright magnets, one under each string. Surrounding each upright magnet is a coil of hundreds of turns of very thin copper wire.

The strings of the electric guitar are all made of metal. When the player sets a string vibrating, the rapid back-and-forth movement changes the magnetic field created by the upright magnet. The vibration in the magnetic field creates a tiny current in the coil. And this current changes, or oscillates, at the exact same speed as the vibrating frequency of the string. To put it another way, the pick-up changes the mechanical motion of the string into a corresponding electrical signal.

A wire carries the electrical signal from the coil to an amplifier, which makes the signal bigger. Finally, the amplified signal goes to a loudspeaker, where the electrical signal is changed back to mechanical motion, in the form of sound waves in the air. Control knobs on the guitar, and sometimes foot pedals, allow the players to adjust the loudness and tone quality of the sound. Players can, of course, also control the loudness by plucking harder or softer. (For a full explanation of amplifiers and loudspeakers, turn to page 141.)

The sounds of all the string instruments come from vibrating strings. Despite their common origin, these instruments can produce an amazing variety of musical effects. The next time you hear the heavenly strains of a harp solo, the soaring excitement of a symphony violin section, the soulful strains of a 'cello melody, or the powerful drive of an amplified electric guitar, think for a moment of how they all grew from the twang of a hunter's bow.

Percussion

Every time you clap your hands, stamp your feet, or tap your fingers, you are using your body as a percussion instrument. A percussion instrument is one that produces its sound when hit or struck. The best known percussion instruments are drums, but there are many others in this group.

The very first musicians probably beat on hollow logs or tightly stretched animal skins. They used their drumming to send signals, to lend rhythm to their work, to give them courage in battle, and to provide exciting rhythms for singing and dancing.

All percussion instruments can be divided into two groups—those that do not produce definite pitches and those that

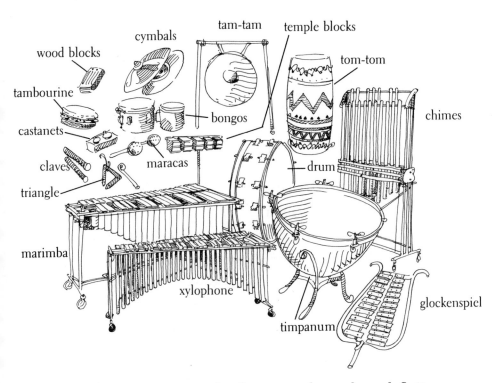

wood blocks · cymbals · tam-tam · temple blocks · tom-tom · tambourine · bongos · chimes · castanets · maracas · drum · claves · triangle · marimba · xylophone · timpanum · glockenspiel

do. The instruments in the first group do not have definite pitch because they vibrate in a complex and irregular way. Their sound waves are jagged and without pattern, in contrast with the more even, repeated sound waves of specific pitches. You might say they produce noise rather than musical tones. Among the most common unpitched instruments are some of the drums and the tambourine, cymbals, tam-tam or gong, triangle, castanets, wood blocks, temple blocks, maracas, and claves.

The percussion instruments that produce definite pitches vibrate regularly, just like the other melodic musical instruments. Their sounds can be identified as particular notes, and their sound waves show a regular, repeated pattern. Timpani or kettledrums, tom-toms, bongos, and the xylophone, marimba, glockenspiel, vibraphone, and chimes are the most familiar pitched percussion instruments.

Drums

Drums come in all sizes and shapes. But every drum has at least two parts in common. There is a head on which the drummer beats. And there is a frame, or shell, to support the drumhead and to reflect and amplify the sound.

One drum you probably know well is the snare drum, or side drum, as it is sometimes called. The snare drum is small—about 15 inches wide and between 5 and 8 inches deep. It has two plastic or calfskin heads. The top head is known as the batter head. The player strikes the batter head with a pair of wooden sticks. The sticks are used to make single strokes, to play patterns of notes, or to play rolls. The roll is a rapid alternation of sticks that can sound like anything from the buzzing of a bee to the roar of a jet plane.

Stretched tightly across the bottom head are the snares—

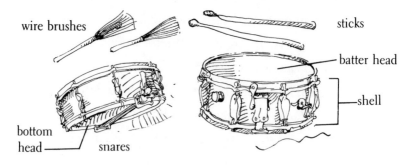

wire brushes   sticks

batter head

shell

bottom head —— snares

strips of gut, nylon, or metal. When the player strikes the batter head, the snares vibrate against the bottom head. The snares actually double the vibrating frequency of the bottom head, creating a very special sharp, crisp sound. If desired, the player can move a lever on the side of the metal or wood shell to loosen the snares. With the snares loosened, the drum has a hollow, dull sound, much like a tom-tom.

Drummers play the snare drum with a pair of hickory-wood sticks that have small, rounded tips. A jazz musician sometimes uses a wire brush, instead of sticks, to keep the beat in soft music. He or she can swish the brush around, creating a gentle rubbing sound, which may be punctuated with occasional slightly firmer strokes.

A close relative of the snare drum is the bass drum. Standard symphony bass drums have a head up to 40 inches across and are 20 inches deep. Like the snare drum, they have two plastic or calfskin heads, but without snares. The bass drum's heads are bigger, as well as thicker and looser. This makes the bass drum generally sound lower in pitch. Players use one or two beaters with soft, felt-covered heads. The drum, usually stood on end, is held by a stand.

The bass drum found in rock groups and jazz bands is much smaller than the one used in orchestras and in parade and concert bands. It rests on the floor, instead of on a stand. To play it the seated drummer steps on a foot pedal, which causes the stick to strike the drumhead. Rock and jazz drummers may play a whole flock of various drums.

Here's how to make your own simple drum. Start with the shell. An empty coffee can, large juice can, or ham tin is fine. Remove both the top and bottom lids and make sure that the can is clean and dry.

Cut open two heavy-paper shopping bags so that they lie flat. Place your shell on one of the bags and trace around the edge. Take the shell away and draw another line about 3 inches beyond the first one. Cut out the larger shape from both bags and paste or glue the two pieces together. That is the drumhead. Stretch your drumhead tightly over the top of the shell and use a heavy rubber band or string to hold it in place.

The drum can be played in several ways. You can strike the head with your fingertips, with the palm of your hand, with a small wooden stick, or with the eraser of a pencil. Each rap will make the drumhead vibrate, making the shell and the air within the shell vibrate. As the sound is reflected back and forth, it becomes louder, giving it a true drum sound.

What about the drums that have both a batter head *and* a bottom head? Even though the drummer does not touch the bottom head, it vibrates when the batter head is struck. Here's how you can prove this. Make another drum head (you'll need only one piece of paper instead of two), but before attaching it to the bottom, toss a few grains of un-cooked rice inside the drum.

Hit the batter head of the drum as before. Do you hear the rice rattling and changing the drum tone? The sound tells you that the bottom head is vibrating too, even though you only struck the batter head. What happens if you leave one lid on the can? Does it affect the loudness? The tone?

Hit, Shake, and Rub

Almost every instrument has changed over the centuries. Yet carvings from 2000-year-old Egyptian tombs picture tambourines that look much like those of today. The modern tambourine has only one head, about 10 inches across, which is nailed to a shallow wooden hoop. Set into the hoop are pairs of tinkly metal discs called jingles.

The tambourine has two sound producers—the plastic or calfskin head and the jingles. The particular sound depends on how it is played. You can hit the head with your knuckles, fingertips, hand, or even your knee, elbow, or head. This gives the percussive sound of the blow, plus the sound of the shaking jingles. You can shake the tambourine. This gives the sound of the jingles, but without the percussive quality. Or you can run your slightly moist thumb around the edge of the head. This gives a fast, trembling jingle sound.

To make your own tambourine, you'll need an old pie tin, twelve shallow, fluted soda-bottle caps, about 20 inches of wire, a hammer, and a large nail. First hammer the bottle caps until they are nearly flat. Then use the hammer and nail to punch six holes around the edge of the pie tin and one in the center of each cap. When you are finished, cut off six 3-inch lengths of wire and tie two caps to each hole.

Try the different ways to play your tambourine. Can you hear how the sound changes with each method?

Cymbals look like two huge gold-colored pot covers. But when the player smashes them together, few can resist the special excitement that comes from their explosive sound.

The cymbals are actually slightly arched, round brass plates that range from 14 to 26 inches in diameter. A leather handle is usually fastened to a small hole at the center of each cymbal. The player holds the cymbals by the strap

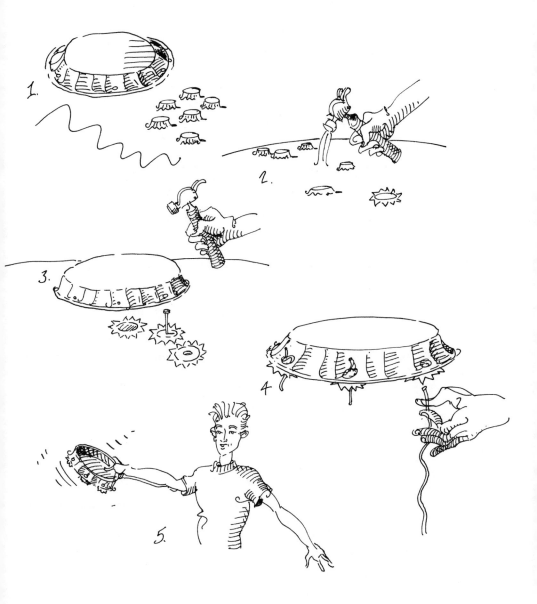

1.

2.

3.

4.

5.

handles and crashes them together with a sliding motion. This creates powerful vibrations in both cymbals. If the player then turns the vibrating cymbals toward the audience, the cymbals actually direct the sound waves straight at the listeners. To stop the vibrations, and the sound, the player pulls the cymbals back tightly against his or her chest.

Players in rock bands and pop groups usually clash their cymbals in a different way. They attach several different-sized single cymbals, called ride cymbals, to the tops of upright metal rods known as cymbal stands. The musician strikes them with a wooden snare-drum stick to outline and punctuate the rhythm of the piece.

A special kind of ride cymbal is the sizzle cymbal. It looks like the other ride cymbals, but produces a high-pitched "sizzle" sound each time it is struck. The sound comes from the vibrations of metal rivets that are set into small holes in the cymbal. A jazz, rock, or pop drummer may also use a pair of small cymbals that are mounted on an upright rod. The drummer then uses a foot pedal to clash these so-called high-hat cymbals together.

The tam-tam, or gong, has among the most dramatic of all instrumental sounds. Its sound has a mysterious quality that brings to mind the music of the Far East. The instrument is made of hammered bronze. It is up to 5 feet across, with a turned-up edge. The player strikes it with a soft, padded beater head. Even though it has no definite pitch, the tam-tam's sound is unique because of its many over-tones. The instrument can be played with a single stroke or with a sustained *tremolo*, in which the player strikes the tam-tam over and over again as fast as possible. (Note that tom-tom is sometimes spelled tam-tam, but a tam-tam is a gong, not a tom-tom!)

The cymbal and tam-tam are alike in one basic way—both are vibrating metal discs. But scientifically they are different. The cymbal's vibrations start at the rim and move in toward the center. The tam-tam's vibrations start at the center and move out.

You can actually see the vibrations in a cymbal-like disc. You'll need a flat metal dish or tray, some fine sand or powder, and a piece of sandpaper. Cover the dish or tray with a thin layer of the sand. Then draw the sandpaper slowly and gently over the edge of the plate.

The rubbing of the rough sandpaper makes the metal vibrate, sending waves through the dish. The metal itself vibrates in a wavelike pattern. At some points it is vibrating freely and shaking the sand away. No sand piles up there. At other points, though, there are nodes, or places with no vibrations. The sand accumulates at these nodes. The resulting pattern looks something like ocean waves, but here it is formed in the sand by the sound waves.

The triangle is simply a steel rod bent to form a three-sided figure about 6 inches long on each side. One corner is left open. The gap allows the vibrations to escape freely into the air without being reflected back through the metal. This free escape of sound adds to the clear, bright tone of the triangle.

The triangle has a sound without definite pitch. Yet if you play the triangle along with a melodic instrument, it seems to pick up the pitch of that instrument. In fact, if you play a scale on a piano and strike the triangle with each note, it sounds as though the triangle is playing the same pitches as the piano.

Players hold the triangle by a short loop of string through one corner and use a short metal beater to set it vibrating. Most often they just make single strokes. Sometimes, though, they go back and forth quickly inside a corner creating a jingling sound, like a bicycle bell, which is called a trill. The triangle's penetrating tone quality allows it to be heard even when an entire band or orchestra is playing.

To add a triangle to your homemade percussion section, simply tie a loop of string through a horseshoe and strike it with a heavy nail.

*　　*　　*

Flamenco dancers (also known as Spanish dancers) often accompany the rhythmic stamping of their feet with the sharp clicking sound of castanets. The performer holds a pair of small wooden clappers tied to the thumb of each hand, and clacks them together with the fingertips to add rhythmic spice to the dance. Usually the pairs of castanets in the player's left and right hand are of different sizes. The larger one makes a lower sound, which represents a man. The smaller pair is higher pitched to signify a woman.

Their name comes from the Spanish *castaña*, which means "chestnut." Castanets usually consist of two pieces of hard chestnut wood, which are hollowed out into spoon shapes and paired with the hollows facing each other. When used in an orchestra, the two pieces are tied to either side of a flat wooden handle. The handle is struck or shaken to produce the special clacking sound.

Today's commercial bands often use another type of castanets, called machine castanets. Machine castanets are mounted horizontally with a spring and a clamp on a hard wooden board. Machine castanets are played by striking them from above with the fingers.

Even though castanet means chestnut, you can make castanets out of a walnut. Open a large walnut very carefully, so that the two halves of the shell are not broken. Then, with caution, remove the nut meat from inside. Drill the smallest hole possible in each shell close to the pointed end. Tie the two shells together loosely with a length of string.

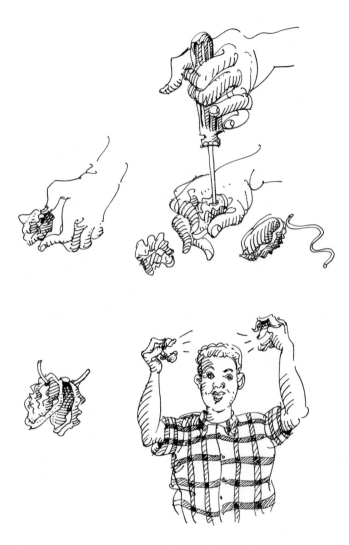

Hook your thumb through the loop of the string so that the shells rest lightly across your palm. Now tighten the string to hold the castanets somewhat open and drum your fingertips on the top one to clack them together. Get another walnut, either larger or smaller than the first, to make another pair for your other hand. Since size determines the pitch, try to hold a conversation between the larger, lower-pitched castanets and the smaller, higher-pitched ones.

As a percussion instrument, the wood block is hardly more than a rectangular block of hard wood. But because a solid wooden block would make a thick, dull sound when struck, there is a slit cut into the wood. The opening adds a resonance and ring to the sound. When played with a hard stick, the wood block produces a distinctive "clop" like the sound of horses' hooves.

Temple blocks are also blocks made of wood, but while the simple wood block has a slit cut into it for resonance, the temple blocks are actually scooped out inside. When struck with a hard stick, the temple blocks give off a distinctive hollow sound. Originally they were used in temple rituals in China and Korea, and were made of hard woods from that part of the world.

The Western temple blocks of today are usually made of maple. Most often in our orchestras or bands a row of brightly colored temple blocks is mounted together on a stand. Although temple blocks do not have definite pitches, the different sizes generally yield a higher or lower sound.

One percussion instrument, the maracas, started out as a hard-shelled fruit called a gourd, which grows on a vine. When the fruit dries out and is shaken, the seeds inside make an attractive rattling sound against the outside shell. The maracas were first played in Latin America, but are now found throughout the world. While some maracas are still made from gourds, today most are made of wood or plastic and contain buckshot.

You can make your own maracas. Clean two empty pint-size milk containers. Put a handful of dried peas or beans inside and glue the lids shut. With a pair of scissors make a small hole in each of two opposite sides of the containers. Push a dowel stick or long pencil through the openings. Use tape to secure the container to the handle. Shake your maracas with sharp, stiff-wrist movements to play any one of the many Latin American dance rhythms.

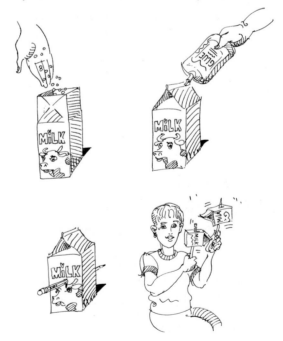

The claves (clah-vehs) hardly look like a musical instrument at all. They are made of two 6-inch lengths of wood—rosewood is best—and are about 1 inch in diameter. The claves are played by hitting one piece of wood against the other. Usually hitting two pieces of wood together gives a dull "thump" sound. But claves, when they are well played, produce wonderfully vibrant "tings" that can point up any dance rhythm.

The magical sound of the claves lies not in the instrument itself but in the way it is played. Musicians hold one clave in the left hand, with the hand as deeply cupped as possible. The other clave is held in the right hand. When the left clave is hit, the cupped hand amplifies the vibrations, creating the sharp, loud sound.

Making your own claves is very simple. Get an old broomstick, cut off two 6-inch lengths, sandpaper them to make them smooth, paint them to make them colorful—and you're in business.

Instruments With Pitch

The idea of making a percussion instrument by stretching a skin over a hollow bowl dates far back in history. Such drums have been known in the Middle East for over 1000 years. Often mounted on horses or camels, they were played by soldiers to frighten the enemy in battle.

The timpani, which are part of every orchestra and most

bands, are the modern form of this instrument. Because the plastic drumhead is often stretched over a big copper or fiberglass bowl that looks like a giant kettle, the timpani are also called kettledrums. (Timpani refers to two or more drums; the singular is timpanum or kettledrum.) Timpani are played with sticks, which range from those with very soft padded heads to those with hard wooden or plastic heads. The timpanist must be able to play single strokes and rhythmic patterns, as well as a thunderlike roll made by rapidly alternating sticks.

Most symphony orchestras use three different timpani, with heads usually about 23, 26, and 29 inches in diameter. Each size gives a different, definite pitch. As you already know, the smaller the head, the higher the pitch, and the larger the head, the lower the pitch. The player can also control the pitch of the timpani. Using either a foot pedal or hand screw, the timpanist can stretch or loosen the head slightly. Tightening, of course, raises the pitch; loosening lowers it.

The rounded bowl of the kettledrum adds resonance to the sound. It also modifies the vibrations so that they produce a specific pitch. At the very bottom of the bowl is a small hole to let the air out. Without the hole, the head might rip apart when a loud note is struck.

One entire family of pitched percussion instruments consists of a series of wooden or metal bars of different lengths mounted together. The science of these instruments is simple. The longer the bar, the lower the pitch; the shorter the bar, the higher the pitch. The best known instruments of this type are the xylophone, marimba, glockenspiel, and vibraphone.

The xylophone has up to forty-eight wooden bars that are arranged in order from short to long. The bars are placed on their frame like the notes on the piano, with the "white" keys in front and the "black" keys behind. Beneath each slab is a hollow tube to add resonance to the sound. The tubes also vary in length, going from short to long, just like the bars above them. The player uses a pair of mallets topped with heads of wood, rubber, or felt to strike the xylophone.

The marimba is little more than a large xylophone. The vibrating bodies are again wooden slabs of different lengths, with a tube beneath each slab to add resonance to the sound. The marimba, though, plays lower and has a wider range of notes than the xylophone. The soft-headed mallets with which it is usually played give the marimba its own special tone. Marimbas are very popular folk instruments in Mexico and Central America. Some marimba bands have two or three players to each instrument.

A xylophone with metal bars instead of wooden ones, and without resonating tubes, is called a glockenspiel. The name means "bell play" in German. Indeed, when struck with a wooden or metal mallet, the glockenspiel produces wonderfully ringing, bell-like tones. In the orchestra the glockenspiel sits flat on a frame. In the marching band the same instrument is held up in front of the player and is called the bell lyra.

Notes sounded by the xylophone, marimba, and glockenspiel do not sustain for very long. As soon as a note is sounded, it begins to fade. Only by hitting a slab with one stick after another very rapidly can the player create the illusion of a held note.

The vibraphone was created around 1916 to sustain the sound of such an instrument. The vibraphone has the metal bars of a glockenspiel, plus the resonating tubes of the xylophone. Each tube, though, is topped by a metal disc that spins around, driven by an electric motor. As the discs spin, they open and close the passages between the bars and the tubes. This adds a trembling quality, or vibrato, to the tone and enables it to continue to sound. By stepping on the pedal beneath the vibraphone, the player is able to control the length of each note.

Although it is sometimes used in an orchestra, the vibraphone is most popular in jazz groups, where it is called "the vibes."

You can make your own homemade xylophone. Get a 7-foot strip of wood about 2 inches wide and 1 inch thick. Mark off eight lengths for the slabs of your xylophone:

12 inches—C	10½ inches—G
11½ inches—D	9¾ inches—A
11 inches—E	9¼ inches—B
10¾ inches—F	9 inches—C

weather stripping

To hold the slabs you'll need a strip of wood 4 feet 2 inches long and about half an inch by half an inch. Cut out two lengths of 20 inches, one of 6 inches, and one of 4 inches, and nail them together to form a long, narrow frame.

Line up the slabs on the floor, about half an inch apart. Place the frame on top of the slabs. On the slabs, draw a line along the two long sides of the frame with a pencil. Now remove the frame and set lengths of weather stripping or felt just inside the two lines. With a hammer and small carpenter's tacks, nail the strips to each of the slabs. Carefully lift the slabs and, with the strips facing the frame, center them on the frame. Tack the ends of the strips to the frame and add a couple of tacks between the slabs.

Play your xylophone with two wooden dowels or with two wooden balls glued to the ends of dowels. See how many different melodies you can pick out on your homemade xylophone.

No list of percussion instruments is complete without a mention of chimes or tubular bells. These are round pipes of different lengths, hung on a rack. They are struck by hammerlike mallets to produce a sound like church bells. And there is the celesta, which looks like a small upright piano. Inside, though, there is a series of different-length metal bars. When the player presses a key on the celesta, a hammer strikes one of the bars, setting it into vibration.

Some consider the piano a percussion instrument, since the sound is produced by hammers striking the strings. Others say that the piano is part of the string family since the strings are the vibrating bodies. Because the piano seems to belong in two different families, and because it is so popular and widely played, we shall devote a separate chapter to this important instrument and its relatives.

Keyboards: Pianos, Organs, Synthesizers

All musical instruments have their own histories, from the most primitive forms to the latest advanced versions. But the story of the development of the keyboard instruments is probably the most fascinating of all.

Ancestors of the Piano and Organ

The oldest pianolike instrument dates back over 2000 years to ancient Greece. It was a type of organ called a *hydraulis*, which used water to control the air blowing through the pipes. Since the *hydraulis* keys were very large and stiff, the players had to bang them down with their fists. They did not press them with their fingers, as in modern keyboard instruments.

During the Middle Ages, an instrument important to the

growth of the piano was brought to Europe from the Middle East. This instrument, which was called a *santir*, had strings of graduated lengths, like the harp. But the *santir* strings were stretched over a sound board that added resonance as players struck them with long, curved hammers.

Two different instruments, the psaltery and the dulcimer, sprang from the *santir* in the fourteenth and fifteenth centuries. The player plucked the strings of the psaltery by hand or with a pick. The dulcimer player, on the other hand, used long, thin hammers to set the strings vibrating.

A modern version of the psaltery is the zither. It has five metal strings which the player presses with his or her thumb to produce the melody while plucking with the other fingers. The zither has forty other strings that are strummed for the accompaniment.

Around the year 1400 an instrument appeared in Europe called the clavichord. In a way, the clavichord was a dulcimer with keys. The clavichord brought together the idea of a keyboard with the idea of striking strings to set them vibrating. Along one side of the rectangular wood clavichord case was the keyboard. Attached to each key was a wooden strip with an upright wedge of brass at the end, called a tangent. Inside the instrument were the strings.

When the player pressed a key, the tangent moved up and struck a string, causing it to sound. As long as the player kept the key down, the tangent remained against the string and the note continued to sound. Players could even wiggle

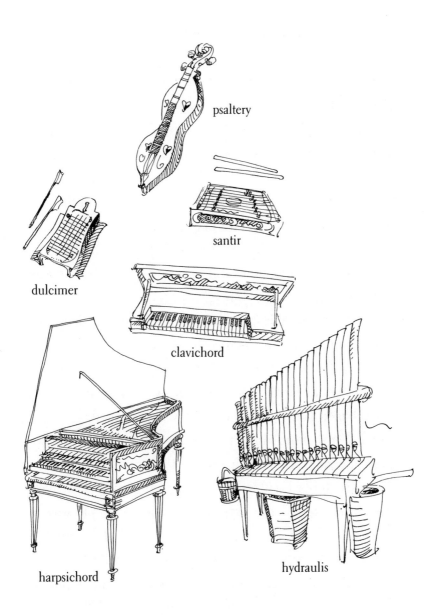

psaltery

santir

dulcimer

clavichord

harpsichord

hydraulis

the keys with their fingers to add an attractive shaking, or vibrato, to the tone.

The harpsichord, which came along a little after the clavichord, can be thought of as a psaltery with keys. The harpsichord, like the clavichord, has a keyboard and strings. But, as with the psaltery, the strings are plucked to make them sound: The keys of the harpsichord are attached to upright pieces of wood called jacks. Near the top of the jack is a small pick. When the player presses a key, the jack moves up and the pick plucks the string. In the past the pick was either a feather quill or a piece of leather. Today it is usually made of nylon.

The harpsichord is the oldest forerunner of the piano that is still popular today. Harpsichord players often perform music that was written before the invention of the piano. A harpsichord looks like a small baby grand piano with a harp-shaped body, often beautifully ornamented.

The harpsichord's bright, clear tone proved very attractive from the start. But the instrument had some drawbacks. The jacks moved with the same force no matter how hard the player pressed the keys. There was no simple way to make notes louder or softer. Also, the sounds of the plucked strings did not sustain; they faded away immediately.

Instrument makers continued looking for an improved keyboard instrument. By the end of the seventeenth century they were experimenting with instruments that resemble the modern piano.

The Piano

Around the year 1709, Bartolomeo Cristofori (1655–1731) of Florence, Italy, built the first true piano. He called it a "harpsichord with soft and loud." Since the Italian for "soft and loud" is *piano e forte*, the instrument became known as a pianoforte, which people have since shortened to piano.

Cristofori's main advances were three. In his new instrument, the strings were set vibrating with soft hammers, rather than tangents or quills as in the older instruments; the new design of the hammer action allowed the player to produce softer or louder tones by using different pressures on the keys; and a special mechanism was included that caused the keys to fall back immediately after striking a string so that notes could be repeated and played rapidly. These features are still the foundation of the wonderful sound of our pianos today.

The strings of the piano are stretched across a frame that looks something like a harp. The lowest strings are long, thick, and loose. The higher strings are short, thin, and tight. This is a practical necessity. If all the strings on the piano were of the same tightness and thickness, the bottom note would need a string 30 feet long, or three times its present length!

By themselves, the piano strings do not produce much sound. For that reason the piano strings pass over a wooden bridge that sits on the soundboard, a heavy piece of wood the size and shape of the body of the piano. The vibrations travel from the string to the bridge and to the soundboard. The big soundboard sends out much stronger sound waves than the strings alone.

All the strings are attached to metal pegs. Although the pegs are tight enough to stay fixed in place, they can be turned to get the strings in tune. Generally this is left to professional piano tuners. Equipped with a special tool called a tuning hammer, the tuner tightens or loosens the pegs to get each note to the proper pitch.

The modern grand piano has a keyboard of eighty-eight black and white keys. Each key is connected to a hammer. The hammers are beneath the strings. (In upright pianos the hammers are in front of the strings.) Made of wood with a felt covering, the hammers are connected to the keys. The linkup between the key and hammer is called the action. When you press the key, the action sends the hammer against the string or strings for that note.

For the lower notes, each hammer strikes one thick, heavy string wound with copper wire. The middle keys strike two strings each. Since these strings are thinner and set less air vibrating, more than one string is needed to produce enough sound. And for each high note there are three strings, since they are the thinnest of all.

If you look inside a grand piano, you will see strips of felt-covered wood sitting on the strings. These are the dampers. The dampers stop the string from vibrating, except

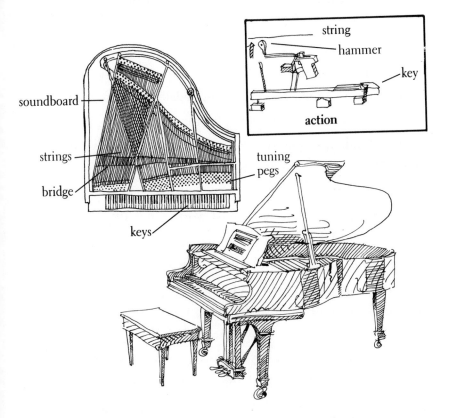

when the player wants that string to sound. They are attached to the keys. Press a key and the damper rises off the string so that it can vibrate. Release the key and the damper falls back on the string and stops the sound.

Most pianos have three pedals. The pedal on the player's right is called the damper pedal, although a better name might be the "un-damper" pedal! Stepping on this pedal raises all the dampers above the strings, no matter what notes are being played. With the dampers up, all the notes that have been played keep on sounding. Players use this pedal to sustain the sound and go smoothly from one note to the next.

The pedal on the player's left is called—correctly—the soft pedal. On grand pianos, the soft pedal moves the hammers slightly sideways. Instead of hitting two or three strings for the middle and high notes, the hammers hit only one or two. With fewer strings sounding, the tone of the piano is naturally softer.

In upright pianos, the soft pedal works differently. Stepping on the pedal moves the hammers closer to the strings, which also makes the sound softer. Think of hammering a nail. You can't hit the nail as hard if you start your stroke with the hammer held just above the nail as you can with the hammer starting far above the nail. In the same way, moving the hammers closer to the strings creates softer sounds.

The middle pedal, called the *sostenuto*, or sustaining pedal, is not found on all pianos. When stepped on, this pedal catches and holds up the dampers of only the notes that you are playing at that moment. This lets you hold out those notes, while the notes that follow stop sounding as soon as you release their keys.

The Tempered Scale

The strings on all keyboard instruments are tuned to particular notes. The first method for tuning was worked out by Pythagoras, the Greek mathematician-musician, around the year 500 B.C. According to Pythagoras the second note of a scale, for example, should have a frequency 9/8 that of the first note. The frequency of the third note should be 10/8 (or 5/4) of the first note. And so on.

Suppose you start the scale on the note middle C, which has a frequency of 256 vibrations per second. Then the next note, D, is pitched at 288 (256 × 9/8 = 288), and the E following is at 320 (256 × 10/8 = 320).

But now, let us say you start the scale on the note D, with a frequency of 288. In this case E proves to be 324 (288 × 9/8 = 324), rather than 320. That is, the note E has a frequency of 320 in the C scale, but 324 in the D scale!

How can you possibly tune a piano if the same note has a different frequency—and therefore pitch—in each scale? Someone figured out that you would need seventy separate strings for each scale to make a piano that could play perfectly in tune. That means you would need over 1000 strings for a standard piano!

As a matter of fact, the old instruments were very badly out of tune, and by around the year 1700 it became clear that a method of tuning was needed that would work for *all* scales. The solution was to multiply a note's frequency by 1.059 to get a frequency of the note a half step higher.

Let's start on the same middle C and see how this works. C is at 256. C sharp (a half step above C) is at 256 × 1.059, or 271.1. D will then be at 271.1 × 1.059, or 287. D sharp will be at 287 × 1.059, or 304. And E will then be at 304 × 1.059, or 322. Compare the frequency of this E with the E of the C scale and the E of the D scale. This E falls in the middle, and is truly a compromise.

This approach is called tempered tuning. The invention

of tempered tuning impressed the famous eighteenth-century German organist and composer Johann Sebastian Bach very much—so much that he wrote a collection of pieces called *The Well-Tempered Clavier*. (Clavier means keyboard.) *The Well-Tempered Clavier* contains forty-eight pieces, two in each of the twenty-four possible keys (twelve major and twelve minor), and all these pieces can be played on the same instrument. Without tempered tuning, most of these pieces would sound out of tune. As it is, they sound beautiful and are still often performed today, on both the harpsichord and the piano.

Today all pianos and other instruments with fixed pitch are tuned to the tempered scale. Although it is a compromise, it still sounds in tune to our ears.

The piano is one of the most popular of all instruments. Because it can produce so many notes at the same time, it always sounds full and complete. The piano also allows the player to achieve a full range of musical effects, from soft, intimate melodies to the thundering sounds of a full orchestra.

The Pipe Organ

With good reason, the pipe organ is often called the "king of instruments." Huge in size, the organ can fill the largest space—be it an elegant concert hall or a towering cathedral—with its mighty tones.

Yet, as big and complicated as it looks, the organ is based on the simplest of scientific principles. There are only three main parts to the instrument.

First, there is a source of wind. In the early organs the wind came from the slaves or servants pumping bellows by hand or foot. The wind was sent into a wind chest, where it was kept under pressure until needed. In modern organs, there is an electric pump that keeps up a steady air pressure.

Second, there are the pipes, the actual sound producers of the organ. They come in all lengths. And as in all instruments, the longer or thicker the pipe, the lower the pitch. There are two basic types of organ pipes. One type has a hole cut in the pipe itself. As the air rushes through, it is cut by the open hole and is set vibrating. This pipe, called a flute pipe, works much like the flute (see page 89). The other type has a metal reed set into the pipe. The moving air causes the reed to vibrate and produce the sound.

Finally, there is the keyboard, or manual, as it is sometimes called. By pressing the keys on the keyboard, the players send the air to the pipe or pipes that they want to sound. (There isn't a pipe for every key; Many notes are made by combining pipes.) In addition to a keyboard, or up to five keyboards in large instruments, many organs also have a pedalboard for the lower notes. The players work this with their feet. They wear special narrow, pointed shoes to press the wooden bars of the pedalboard, which is located beneath the bench they sit on.

Organists can get many different effects by adjusting the various knobs and levers, called stops, which surround the keyboards. Pull out one stop, and various pipes are combined to make the organ sound like a piano. Other stops produce sounds like violins, flutes, trumpets, or even the human voice. The player can also control the volume, producing any level from softest whisper to loudest shout. This is done by using particular stops. Pressing the separate "swell" pedals makes the sound grow gradually louder or softer.

Between the several keyboards, pedalboard, and various stops, the organist can produce an amazing range of notes and tone colors. In concert, the pipe organ truly reigns over all other instruments!

Electric and Electronic Organs

In the late 1930s, Laurens Hammond, an American inventor, devised a small electric organ for home use. The Hammond organ has no pipes. Instead, an electric motor turns a shaft containing ninety-one metal discs. Each disc has a different number of teeth, or bumps, on its edge. And each is always spinning at a constant speed near a magnet wrapped with a wire coil. As the bumps pass near the magnet, they create tiny bursts of electricity in the coil. The more bumps on the wheel, the greater the number of bursts of electricity per second. The fewer the bumps, the less frequent the bursts of electricity. When the player presses a key, it selects one particular frequency and that note sounds.

The speed of these electrical pulses in the electric organ is the same as the speed of vibration in other musical instruments. For example, the note middle C is produced when anything vibrates 256 times a second. The vibrations can be those of a violin string, a clarinet reed, or a trumpeter's lips. Or they can be 256 on/off bursts of electricity in an electric organ. The difference is that you hear the violin, clarinet, or trumpet note as it is being produced. The organ's electrical pulses must first be changed into sound (see pages 141–145).

In the late 1940s, the Baldwin Piano Company manufactured the first electronic organ. Electronic circuits in the instrument produce oscillating electrical currents of any frequency depending on what keys the player presses. This kind of organ produces sound solely by electronic means, without using spinning discs or other moving parts.

Over the years, the electronic organ has been vastly improved. Its sound today closely resembles that of a pipe organ, and the player can push stops to add overtones to imitate any of the other instruments or voices. Among its special features are its ability to provide harmony, chords, and rhythm for any melody and to store whatever is played in its memory. Performing on a modern electronic organ is a little like conducting a full electronic symphony orchestra!

The Synthesizer

The synthesizer is a twentieth-century musical instrument that is like the electronic organ—but much, much more! The instrument is played on a pianolike keyboard. Above and to the sides of the keyboard are a large number of controls, switches, and dials. Beneath the keyboard and controls is a box of electronic circuitry. Since most of the circuits are etched on tiny chips, an amazing amount of electronics can be squeezed into this small box.

Each synthesizer is made up of five basic parts—the source of the signals, signal modifiers, a control system, mixers, and output.

The signal generator provides the on/off flow of electricity at any frequency to produce signals at any desired pitch.

The signal modifiers change the basic signal to suit the taste of the player. They can make the sound louder or

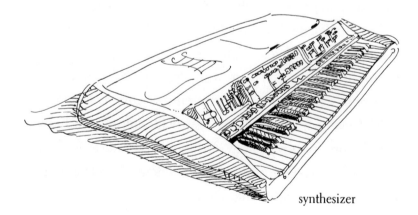

synthesizer

softer; they can add overtones or take them away; they can shape the sound wave to imitate just about any sound, musical or not.

The control system directs the operation of the synthesizer. In most electronic devices, the control system is a series of switches. But since the synthesizer is a musical instrument, many of the switches are built into the keyboard. A person can "play" the synthesizer just like a piano. Pressing a key is the same as flipping a switch. The player presets the synthesizer to have each key produce the exact signal he or she wants.

The mixers combine several electronically created signals. By joining two or more signals, the synthesizer can sound like a small group or even a large orchestra and can achieve a variety of special musical effects.

From the mixers, the signal goes to the output. Sometimes the synthesizer is played "live," just like any other musical instrument. In this case, the signal goes to an amplifier and loudspeaker. Or the synthesizer can be used to record directly on tape. When this happens, the signal passes directly to a connected tape recorder. With a monitor, the person using the synthesizer can hear the sounds.

Most synthesizers have special built-in features that allow them to do some amazing things. For instance, there is often a "glide" control that lets you move smoothly from note to note. You can also preset the exact way that a note starts to sound and how it decays or fades away. This is called the "envelope" of the sound. By shaping the envelope in specific ways, you can imitate the sound of any instrument or voice, or create new and exciting sounds.

The shape of the sound wave is under the synthesizer player's control as well. A smooth sine wave produces a flutelike sound. For an oboe, a sawtooth wave is best. And to sound like a clarinet, a square wave does the trick. Special filters can remove any unwanted frequencies. And finally, the synthesizer has a memory that can store several separate lines of music and play them back together or separately.

Most synthesizers have tiny computers, called microprocessors, in their electronic circuits. The microprocessors control the many different operations of the synthesizer. Some of the more advanced synthesizers can also be hooked up to outside computers. Through such an outside computer you can feed information directly to the synthesizer.

In writing a song, the composer can enter the melody in the computer. The computer will then generate the chords and rhythm. If the music you want to play is too fast or too difficult, you can enter each note slowly in the computer. With a push of a button (players call this "invisible fingers"), the computer will enter it into the synthesizer at the right speed. For movie or television scores, the synthesizer can synchronize the film and the music. Among its other marvels, the synthesizer can show you the sound waves you are creating—and even print out an entire score of music for you!

The synthesizer is more than an amazing instrument. It also represents a brilliant outcome of the joining of science and music. Much music composed today—from rock concerts to background music for television and movies—includes a synthesizer. In fact, the synthesizer is being used so widely that it is putting many professional musicians out of work!

Woodwinds

The woodwind instruments include the flute, oboe, clarinet, saxophone, bassoon—and all of their relatives. Originally all were made of wood (today some are made of metal) and are all played by blowing, hence the name woodwind.

Have you ever blown across the top of an empty soda bottle and heard a low, hooting sound? If so, you produced a sound in much the same way as a musician playing one kind of woodwind instrument! As you blew, your breath was cut by the opposite side of the bottle top. Some went out into the air. But the rest went down into the bottle and set the air in there vibrating. As the sound waves bounced around inside the bottle, they produced a sound like a low,

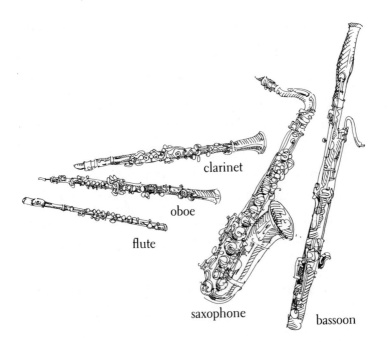

clarinet

oboe

flute

saxophone

bassoon

soft boat whistle. The flute works on the soda-bottle principle.

Have you ever held a blade of grass between your thumbs,
blown on it, and produced a high, piercing whistle? This
is also a type of primitive woodwind instrument. The stream
of air from your mouth sets the blade of grass vibrating.
The clarinet, saxophone, oboe, and bassoon are instruments
of the blade-of-grass type.

The Sound of Woodwinds

All woodwinds are basically long tubes. Their sound comes
from the vibrating column of air within the tube. And the

length and thickness of the vibrating column determine the pitch. If the vibrating column is long and wide, the pitch is low. A short, narrow vibrating column produces a high pitch.

You can try this out with four one-liter empty soda bottles. Leave Bottle 1 empty. Put a little less than 2 cups of water in Bottle 2, 2¾ cups of water in Bottle 3, and 3¾ cups of water in Bottle 4.

Blow across each in turn. Which has the highest pitch? Which, the lowest? Bottle 4 is highest because it has the shortest air column. Bottle 1 is lowest for the opposite reason; its air column is longest.

Now line Bottles 1, 2, 3, and 4 along the edge of a kitchen counter or a table. Blow across the tops in this order: 1, 1, 2; 1, 2, 3; 1, 2, 3; 1, 2, 3; 1, 2, 3; 2, 3, 4; 3, 2, 1; 1, 1, 2. Did they sound the bugle call "Taps"? You may have to "tune" them. If a note sounds too high, spill out some water. If a note sounds too low, add a little.

See if you can play other melodies with your bottles. If you want to add notes, collect more bottles and fill them with other levels of water.

According to ancient Greek legend, the first woodwind was the "pipes of Pan." The god Pan was a happy, ugly man with horns, beard, tail, and goat's feet, who loved to chase beautiful women. One day he pursued the nymph (female spirit) Syrinx. But her friends, the water nymphs, saved Syrinx by changing her into a tall reedlike plant. Pan hugged the reed and sighed sadly, producing a musical sound from the reeds. Pan cut the reed into several different lengths and tied them together. He blew across the tops to play melodies that reminded him of his beloved.

Obviously, the pipes of Pan were limited to playing pieces that used few notes. In time, someone got the idea of drilling a row of holes along the length of one pipe. In this way, a single pipe could produce a whole range of notes.

If the player covers all the holes with fingers, the vibrating column of air is as long as the tube. The pitch is low. But what happens if the player uncovers the hole farthest along the tube? The air escapes at that point. That shortens the vibrating column and the pitch goes up. As the player shortens the column hole by hole, the pitch goes higher and higher. Lengthening or shortening the vibrating column of air makes it possible to produce many different notes on a single tube.

But woodwind players wanted to be able to play even more notes. Eventually they learned to add notes by cross-fingering. The idea of cross-fingering is to leave one hole open between covered holes.

Suppose, for example, the player covers Holes 1, 2, 3, and 4, leaves Hole 5 open, and covers Holes 6, 7, and 8. Some air escapes through the open hole (Hole 5 in our example). This creates a point of no vibration, which changes the length of the sound wave, and changes the pitch. Opening Hole 5 actually produces a different note than leaving all eight holes covered.

The player can also add notes by blowing harder into the instrument. This technique, called overblowing, may also require the player to press a special key. Overblowing causes the pitch to jump up to the first overtone instead of sounding the basic note. The first overtone is eight notes, or an octave, higher than the basic note. Thus, overblowing makes the note sound an octave higher.

Blowing even harder produces pitches that are two octaves higher than the basic note. (This usually requires opening some extra holes on the tube.) With overblowing, the player can triple the number of basic notes that most woodwind instruments can play!

You can try to overblow on your bottle. First produce a basic tone the same way as before. Now blow harder and faster. Make an extremely narrow stream of air with your tightened lips. Do you hear the pitch jump up?

Jumping up an octave by overblowing works for all the woodwind instruments except the clarinet. When the clarinet is overblown it jumps to the second overtone (an octave plus four notes above the basic note). We shall see why this happens when we talk about the clarinet on page 92.

The final way to add notes on woodwinds is through the use of keys. The keys are usually thin metal rods and levers with round, cup-shaped ends. Inside the cup is a soft pad that can cover a hole just as well as a finger. The keys can also cover holes that cannot be reached with a finger, cover several holes at one time, cover holes that are larger than the size of a finger, and make it easier to go rapidly from note to note.

The Flute

The modern flute is a metal tube just over 26½ inches long. The instrument is usually made in three sections—head, middle, and foot joints. The head joint contains the mouth hole, a large opening with a raised collar around it. The middle and foot joints have a jumble of holes and keys along their lengths.

The player holds the flute horizontally under the bottom lip and blows across the mouth hole. The sharp edge of the mouth hole cuts the stream of air, sending some into the flute. Splitting the stream of air sets the column of air inside the instrument vibrating, producing the flute sound. By opening and closing the holes along the tube, the player raises and lowers the pitch.

Most professional flutists play on instruments made of silver. A few use gold or even platinum flutes. The flutes played by beginning students are usually made of nickel silver, which is a silver-white mixture of copper, zinc, and nickel with no silver in it.

Many flutists believe that gold flutes sound better than those made of nickel silver or silver. But some scientists are not so sure. These scientists point out that it is the air inside the flute that vibrates. The tube itself hardly vibrates at all.

Therefore, the material of the tube should not make any difference in the sound.

Why then do flutists find that gold flutes sound better? Probably because more care is taken in the manufacture of gold flutes than with those made of nickel silver. The more precisely the instrument is made, the clearer its tone, the better its tuning, and the easier it is to play.

The person who gets most credit for creating the modern flute is the German flutist and instrument maker Theobald Böhm (1794–1881). Between 1830 and 1847, Böhm set a standard for flute making that still holds today. Böhm made his flutes of silver, since he believed it produced the best sound. He created the conical head joint—narrow at the closed end and growing wider through its length—and the cylindrical middle and foot joints with the same bore, or width, throughout. And he invented a key system that allows players to cover and open the holes easily and to change quickly from note to note. Today's flutes are basically Böhm flutes.

The smaller "kid sister" of the flute is the piccolo. The name comes from the Italian *flauto piccolo*, or "little flute." Slightly less than half the length of the flute, the piccolo is pitched exactly an octave higher. Its clear, piercing sound easily penetrates the loudest band or orchestra.

Some piccolos are made of metal, but many are made of wood. *Grenadilla*, the preferred wood, comes from a tree that grows in the Congo Basin in Africa. This heavy, hard,

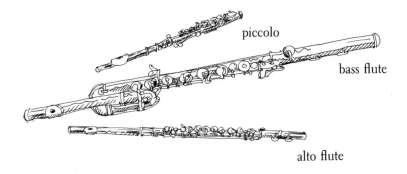

piccolo

bass flute

alto flute

dark-brown wood can be polished to a very bright shine.

The flute also has two "big sisters"—the alto flute and bass flute. Both are longer and slightly wider than the standard flute. The alto flute was invented by Böhm. About 8 inches longer than the standard flute, it plays three notes lower. The bass flute is the latest addition. The first one was built around 1930. Since its tube is nearly double the length of the standard flute, its range is lower by one octave. Because the bass flute is so long, if it were straight it would be impossible for the player to reach all the holes and keys. The tube, therefore, is made in the shape of the letter J. This puts all the holes within the player's reach.

The recorder is a very close relative of the flute and is sometimes called an end-blown flute. The player blows through a simple mouthpiece. A sharp edge cut in the tube, called a window, sets the breath into vibration. Recorders come in a few sizes, ranging from the short sopranino through the larger soprano, alto, and tenor to the largest, the bass.

The Clarinet

The clarinet player produces tones by blowing air past a reed. The reed is made from cane, a kind of wild grass like bamboo, which grows up to 20 feet tall. (Its scientific name is *Arundo donax*.) The stalks are hollow on the inside but have a hard outer shell.

Although cane is found all around the Mediterranean Sea, those plants that grow in southeastern France are preferred by reed makers. The cane plants are cut when they are about two years old. They are then dried, cleaned, and shaped into flat clarinet reeds.

The musician attaches the reed to the mouthpiece of the clarinet, which is usually made of plastic. A metal clamp holds the reed tightly against the opening in the flat bottom of the mouthpiece. When the player blows into the opening, the reed vibrates and produces the full, rich clarinet tone.

Basically the clarinet is a 26-inch-long cylindrical tube with a mouthpiece at one end and a bell-shaped opening

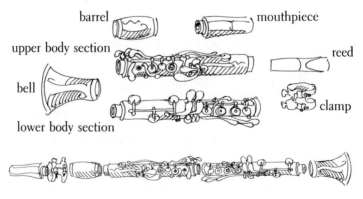

at the other end. As with the piccolo, this instrument is made from the heavy, durable, easily polished African blackwood, *Grenadilla*. For ease in handling, the clarinet is made in five separate pieces.

The barrel is the short length of tubing that connects the mouthpiece to the rest of the instrument. In the past, clarinets came with a few barrels of different lengths, which changed the pitch of the entire instrument. Now there is a standard length, and most clarinets are pitched in B flat.

Beneath the barrel are the upper and lower joints. These are the longest sections; they contain all the holes and keys that are used to play the clarinet. The short bell at the far end sends the warm, smooth clarinet sound out into the air.

As the reed vibrates against the mouthpiece, it is actually opening and closing the end of the tube many times per second. Because of its cylindrical bore (the same diameter from mouthpiece to bell), the clarinet produces its sound differently from the way the flute (with its conical head joint) does.

The vibrating reed makes the clarinet work like a closed tube. The clarinet's pitch is lower than that of an open pipe of the same length. For example, the clarinet and the flute are almost the same length. Yet the closed-pipe clarinet plays six notes lower than the open-pipe flute. That is because the note produced in a closed-pipe tube has a wave length four times the length of the tube. But an open-pipe tube produces a wave only twice the tube length.

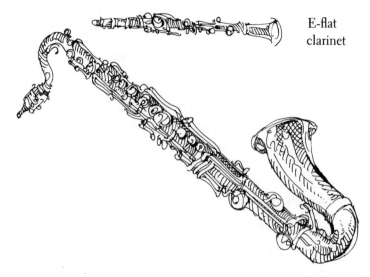

E-flat
clarinet

bass clarinet

The closed pipe creates one more difference. You know that when you overblow an open pipe, the note jumps to the first overtone, which is an octave above the basic note. But when you overblow a closed pipe, it jumps to the second overtone, which is an octave plus four notes.

Clarinets are available in several sizes. The common, standard clarinet, as we said, is the B flat. The A clarinet is almost identical. It is just one inch longer and plays one note lower. The A clarinet is used for music that is difficult or awkward to play on the B-flat clarinet.

The E-flat clarinet, or E-fer as it is called, is the shortest and highest pitched of the clarinets. Its top note is three notes higher than that of the B-flat instrument. At the opposite end of the spectrum is the largest clarinet, the bass clarinet. The bass clarinet is so long, about 4 feet, that it would be impossible to hold if it were a straight tube. Both ends of the instrument, the mouthpiece and the bell, are curved to make it easier to play. The notes of the bass clarinet sound an octave beneath those of the B-flat clarinet.

The clarinet usually serves as the leading instrument in military, marching, and concert bands. In the symphony orchestra it plays an important part, and it sometimes serves as a solo instrument.

The Saxophone

Around the year 1840 a Belgian-born instrument maker, Adolphe Sax (1814–1894), decided to create a new instrument. He wanted it to fill the gap in sound between the

baritone saxophone

tenor saxophone

soprano saxophone

clarinet, a woodwind instrument, and the trumpet, a brass instrument.

In 1846 Sax patented an instrument having a reed, like the clarinet, and a brass body, like the trumpet. He named it the saxophone. The patent described a family of fourteen different instruments, varying in size to cover the entire range of pitches. Five of these saxophones are still in common use—soprano, alto (the most popular), tenor (also popular), baritone, and bass.

Saxophones are curved at both ends like the bass clarinet. The only exception is the soprano saxophone, which is straight like the standard clarinet. But unlike the clarinet, the soprano saxophone is made of brass and is conical (grows wider from mouthpiece to bell).

Even though it is always made of metal, the saxophone resembles other woodwind instruments. Its vibrations are produced by a reed clamped to the mouthpiece. The vibrating body is the column of air in the tube of the instrument. The length and thickness of the tube determine the pitch. Cross-fingerings add extra notes. There is an octave key which the player presses to help produce the higher notes when overblowing. And the saxophone overblows at the octave.

From the very beginning, the saxophone has held a prominent place in military bands. Since then, it has also become widely used in concert bands, dance bands, jazz groups, and even in some works for symphony orchestra.

The Oboe

Just before the start of every orchestra concert, you hear the sound of the oboe. The player is giving out the note A to which all the other instruments tune. The oboe has this job for two reasons. It stays pretty much in tune itself. And its clear, penetrating tone is easy for the other players to hear and to match with their own instruments.

The oboe is a double-reed instrument. Its sound is produced by two reeds vibrating against each other.

A professional oboe player usually makes his or her own reeds out of a narrow strip of cane just over 2 inches long. The cane is folded over and the two ends are tied with thread to a narrow metal tube. Next, the fold is snipped and the reeds are shaped with a knife to the desired size and thickness. When ready to play, the player wets the reeds, either in the mouth or in a small cup of water, and slips the metal tube into the top opening of the oboe.

Here is a quick, simple way to make your own double reed. Flatten one end of a drinking straw and cut in diagonally from both sides to make a point. Hold the pointed end quite tightly with your lips and blow through the straw. The points of the straw act as a double reed and vibrate against each other. That causes the buzz you hear. The vibrating reeds also set the air inside the straw vibrating.

You can test the effect of length on pitch this way. Snip off about an inch of the straw at the straight end. What happens to the pitch? It rises, because the vibrating column of air inside the straw is shorter.

Most modern oboes are made of *grenadilla*, the same hard wood used for clarinets and some piccolos. The 24-inch-long tube has a conical bore, growing gradually wider from the top to the slight bell at the end. Like that of all woodwinds, the pitch is controlled by opening and closing holes along its length. The oboe has its own system of keys and cross-fingerings to obtain all the necessary notes, and it overblows at the octave.

Early in the eighteenth century a larger, lower-pitched oboe was invented that developed into the English horn. This ancestor was called the *oboe da caccia*, Italian for "oboe of the hunt." Since it was curved in shape, the French called it *cor anglé*, meaning "angled horn." But the French word for angled *(anglé)* sounded very much like their word for English *(anglais)*. In time this instrument came to be called the English horn. Curiously enough, the English horn is neither a horn (which is a brass instrument) nor English!

Slightly longer than the oboe, about 30 inches long to the oboe's 24, the English horn plays four notes lower.

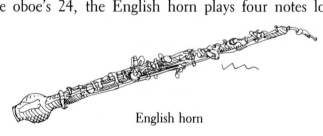

English horn

Although they are closely related, the English horn differs from the oboe in two ways. Because the extra length would make it awkward to play as a straight tube, the English horn's double reed is attached to a bent metal tube. This makes it easier for the player to reach all the keys. Also, the bell is pear shaped, which gives the English horn a slightly softer sound than the oboe.

The Bassoon

The bassoon is the lowest-pitched member of the woodwind family. The sound producer is a double reed, which classifies it as a bass oboe. But the bassoon reed is shorter and heavier than that of the oboe. For its low range, two octaves beneath the oboe, the bassoon tubing is 8½ feet long. The tube, though, is doubled over, making the instrument just over 4 feet long.

To fit into a case that the player can carry, the bassoon can be separated into five parts. A curved metal tube, called the crook, connects the reed to the body of the instrument. The crook slips into the wing, which is the descending part of the bassoon tube. At the bottom is the double joint or butt, in which the tube bends back on itself in a U shape. The long joint is the ascending section of tubing. And the bell, with its slight bulge in the middle, is an extension of the long joint.

Bassoons are made of wood, usually maple or rosewood.

To help support the weight, players usually sit on a strap that they hook onto the instrument.

Because of the great distances between the holes, the keys are particularly important on the bassoon. They make it possible for all players, no matter the size of their hands, to cover all the holes.

The tubing is conical; when the bassoon is overblown, the pitch jumps up an octave. The bassoon has one of the widest ranges of notes of all the instruments. Even though the sound is produced by a double reed, the bassoon has a characteristic sound that is quite different from that of the oboe. Composers often write bassoon parts that evoke humor or comedy.

The largest and lowest of all woodwind instruments is the contrabassoon, which has a tube about 16 feet long. Nearly twice the length of the bassoon, the contrabassoon plays an octave lower. The very long tubing is doubled over four times. Obvious differences between the bassoon and contrabassoon are that the contrabassoon's bell is often made of metal (usually high-quality nickel or silver) and it always points down. Despite the lower pitch, different bell, and bulkier look, the contrabassoon works on the same scientific principles as the bassoon.

As you have seen, every member of the woodwind family is part of a small group within the larger family. The flute group includes the piccolo and the alto and bass flutes. The

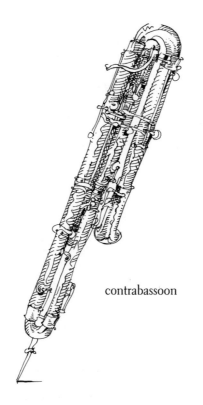

contrabassoon

clarinet family has B-flat, A, E-flat, and bass clarinets. Saxophones come in soprano, alto, tenor, baritone, and bass sizes. The oboe is closely related to the English horn. And the bassoon resembles the contrabassoon.

Each family of woodwinds is played in pretty much the same way. Most players of woodwinds, therefore, can "double" or play two or more instruments. Flutists play piccolo, oboists play English horn, clarinetists play all the clarinets, and so on. But despite the similarity of the members of the various woodwind families, each instrument has its own distinctive sound and character.

CHAPTER SEVEN

Brasses

The ancestors of the brass instruments have sounded their brilliant calls across all the centuries of human history. The very first instruments were made from hollow tree branches and spiral seashells. Later, animal horns were used. It is believed that Moses sounded the *shofar,* a ram's horn, when he led the Jews out of Egypt 4000 years ago. Fifteen hundred years later the Greeks held contests at their Olympics for players of the *salpinx,* a straight trumpet of metal. Night watchmen in ancient Rome sounded the hours on the *buccina,* a relative of the modern tuba. And around the ninth century, the seafaring Vikings sent signals from ship to ship on a type of trumpet.

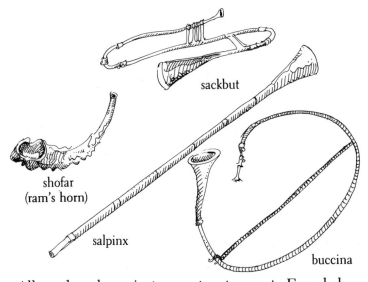

sackbut

shofar
(ram's horn)

salpinx

buccina

All modern brass instruments—trumpet, French horn,
trombone, and tuba—are made of brass. Brass is an alloy,
or mixture, of copper and zinc. The brass is formed into a
long tube with a mouthpiece at one end and a bell at the
other. Every brass instrument produces its sound in much
the same way.

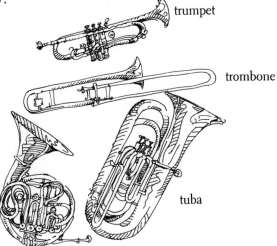

trumpet

trombone

tuba

French horn

The Basic Brass Sound

The sound in all brass instruments starts with the vibration, or buzz, of the player's lips. You can buzz your lips like a brass player. First, though, you must learn the correct embouchure, or lip position. Keep your lips firmly together. Imagine that they are fastened to your teeth, but not curled over. Now, tighten the corners of your mouth and send a blast of air through your lips. Try it a few times. Do you hear a buzz caused by the lips vibrating against each other? If you pulled a brass instrument away from a player's lips in the middle of a note, this is the sound you would hear.

The faster your lips vibrate, the higher the pitch of the buzz. You can raise the basic pitch of your vibrating lips in several ways. You can tighten your lips. You can blow harder. Or you can raise your tongue, making a narrower pathway for the air so that it flows more quickly.

Of course, doing the opposite will make your lips vibrate more slowly and lower the pitch. Relax your lips. Slow down and broaden the flow of air. Do you hear the pitch drop with the slower vibrations?

Brass-instrument players blow through a mouthpiece. But don't let its name fool you. The mouthpiece doesn't go into the player's mouth. It is held against the outside of the player's lips. The mouthpiece shapes and supports the embouchure as the player buzzes into the instrument.

Before they play, brass players get their instruments in tune. They tune by means of a tuning slide. This is a loop or bend in the tubing. If the pitch is too high, they pull out the slide. This lengthens the tubing and lowers the pitch slightly. If the pitch is too low they push in the slide, shortening the tubing and raising the pitch a bit. This tunes all the instrument's pitches down or up together—it is not possible to tune individual notes.

When the player's warm breath strikes the cold metal of the tubing, the moisture condenses. Little drops of water form inside the instrument. If too much water accumulates, the instrument sounds rough and bubbly. The brass instruments have little keys—actually "lids" on springs—that are opened to drain the collected water. They should be called water keys. But almost everyone calls them spit keys.

Sometimes you will see brass players remove a whole loop of tubing from an instrument and shake it out. That is to get rid of water that can't easily be removed through the water key. You can always tell where the brass players sat during a concert because of the wet spots under their seats!

Brass players use devices called mutes to soften or change the tone quality of their instruments. Set into the bell, a mute prevents the instrument from vibrating in the usual way. Mutes are made of many different materials including metal, plastic, and fiberboard.

If you have a balloon, you can make a musical toy and

also see how vibrations produce a buzz in brass instruments. Blowing up the balloon is like filling your lungs with air before playing a brass instrument. Opening the neck of the filled balloon and letting the air rush out is like making a buzz with your lips.

You can change the pitch of the balloon's basic buzz this way. Remember the experiments on page 22? Stretch the opening as you buzz. Does the pitch go up or down? Loosen the opening. What happens to the pitch? Can you play a simple tune by tightening and loosening the balloon opening?

Imagine a brass player making a very low-pitched buzz into any one of the brass instruments. The buzz forms a sound wave within the instrument's column of air. The wave is, of course, invisible, but if you could see it, the wave would look like a jump rope being turned by two people—very wide in the middle and hardly moving at the two ends.

Now think of the player gradually tightening the lips and raising the pitch of his or her buzzing. At first there is no change in the note produced by the brass instrument. Then suddenly the note jumps up in pitch. The original wave has split in half. There are now two shorter sound waves for each original one in the column of air. You can picture this as someone grabbing the center of the jump rope, while the people continue turning it from both ends. It is not moving at the middle and the two ends, but is wide in between. As this happens, the pitch of

the note jumps up to the next overtone of the basic note.

The early brass instruments could leap only several notes at a time, to the next overtone. They could not move up or down by scale step. The bugle is an example of an instrument that is still played in that way. That's why such well-known bugle calls as "Taps," "Reveille," and "Mess Call" jump from note to note.

The early instrument makers knew that changing the length of the tube would give them all the missing notes. The problem was to find practical ways to make the tubing longer or shorter while playing. Their solution can be found in the modern family of brass instruments.

The Trombone

As early as the fourteenth century, brass instruments were built with very long tubing in order to play low notes. To make it easy to handle, the tubing was doubled over into a loop. The idea of building part of this loop as a separate piece that fit over the rest of the tubing, like a tight sleeve over an arm, came a little later. Players could then push out the loop to lengthen the tubing and lower the pitch, or pull it in to shorten the length and raise the pitch. This idea was applied in the first trombone, which was called a sackbut.

The tubing of the modern trombone is bent twice and ends in a flared bell. Trombone players can move the loop, called the slide, to change the length of the tube. The slide actually has seven different positions. Each position gives a different tube length and, thus, basic note. At each position, the player can change the embouchure to get the tones of that basic note's overtone series. In this way, trombonists can play all the different notes on the one instrument.

A trombonist holds the instrument with the left hand and uses the right hand to move the slide in and out. A player may put cold cream or water on the slide to be sure it moves easily. Some trombones have even been built with valves instead of a slide. But valves, most players feel, destroy the true character of the instrument.

Between the cup-shaped mouthpiece and the bell at the

far end, the cylindrical tubing extends almost the entire length of the trombone. The cylindrical bore gives the trombone its majestic, dignified tonal quality.

Two types of trombones are commonly used in orchestras and bands today: the high-pitched tenor trombone, which is nearly 9 feet long, and the lower-pitched bass trombone, which is 2 feet longer.

The Trumpet

The early trumpets were not at all like the first trombones. They were built with different lengths of tubing, called crooks, which could be put in or taken out of the instrument. Put in a longer crook and you lower the basic note and all the overtones. Use a shorter crook and you raise the basic note and all the overtones. But either way, you still could not play all the notes of the scale.

At the beginning of the nineteenth century, the trumpet-type instruments were much improved by the new practice of building the crooks permanently into the tubing. To use the crooks, which lengthened the total length of the tubing, a valve was added to each.

Every modern trumpet, French horn, and tuba has three crooks and three valves. Any of the three valves can be either open or closed; each combination of open and closed valves gives the instrument a different basic note and thus a different overtone series. By switching rapidly from one

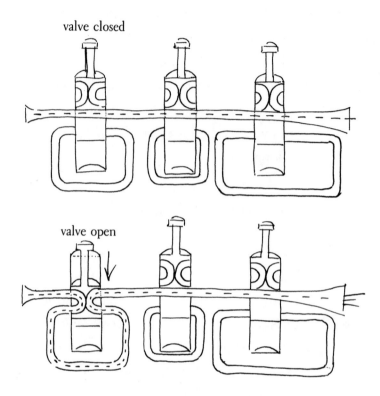

valve closed

valve open

valve position to another, as well as changing embouchure and blowing strength, a trumpeter can play all the notes of any scale or any other sequence of notes that he or she wants to play.

Pressing (or opening) valve No. 1 sends air through a crook that lowers the pitch a whole tone. Pressing the second valve moves the air through a crook half as long as that for No. 1, so it lowers the pitch only half a tone. And pressing the third valve sends the air through a crook as long as the first and second added together. Therefore, opening No. 3 lowers the pitch a full tone and a half.

The seven valve positions of the trumpet, French horn, and tuba correspond to the seven slide positions of the trombone. The seven different combinations of open and closed valves are: No valves at all; valve No. 1 only; No. 2 only; No. 3 only; Nos. 1 and 3; Nos. 2 and 3; or Nos. 1,2, and 3. (The combination of No. 1 and No. 2 is the same as just No. 3.) With these built-in lengtheners, the trumpet and its relatives are flexible, versatile modern instruments.

The modern trumpet gets its clear, brilliant tone from its 53 inches of cylindrical brass tubing, which is doubled over into a loop. To play the instrument, the trumpeter holds the instrument in the left hand and uses the right-hand fingertips to press the valves.

Most symphony orchestras include trumpets, as do almost all bands—concert, military, dance, and jazz. Occasionally trumpets other than the standard one, which is in the key of B flat, are used. The smaller D trumpet and piccolo B-flat trumpet are called for when the music is pitched high. When the composer indicates a trumpet of lower pitch, the player uses the larger bass trumpet.

The cornet looks almost exactly like the trumpet. Hard to see is the difference in its tubing. The cornet's tubing is conical; the trumpet's is cylindrical. Its conical tubing gives the cornet a sweeter, more rounded tone. Very popular as a solo instrument, the cornet is heard more in bands and jazz groups than in symphony orchestras.

The French Horn

Many consider the French horn the most difficult of all instruments to play well. One reason is that the instrument plays mostly in the upper part of the overtone series. The higher you go in the overtones, the closer in pitch the notes become. With notes so close together, the player must have very fine lip and breath control to get each note exactly right. It is very easy to hit the note just above or below by mistake.

The French horn has 12 to 16 feet of tubing wound into a coil. The tube starts at the narrow, funnel-shaped mouthpiece and gradually widens throughout its length until it opens into the graceful 14-inch-wide bell. From its great length of tubing and its slightly conical bore, the French horn gets its deep, rich, broad tone quality.

The French horn has three built-in crooks and three valves. By opening and closing the valves and varying the embouchure, the French hornist can play all the notes of a scale or any other sequence of notes.

The latest development in French horn design makes the instrument even more flexible. The modern type of French horn, called the double horn, has not one complete coil of tubing but two—the usual one with the basic tone of F and a second one with a basic tone of E flat. The two tubes are welded side by side but are not connected. A fourth valve, allows the player to blow into one tube or the other.

The French horn has several musical personalities. Sometimes the French horn can be played to sound strong and powerful, fitting in with the other brass instruments. At other times, though, it can be played to sound just like a woodwind instrument. The warm and mellow tone of the French horn blends so well with wind instruments that it makes up part of the standard woodwind quintet, along with the flute, oboe, clarinet, and bassoon. In the modern orchestra, the French horn players usually number four or five.

The French horn player is the only player of a valved brass instrument who presses the valves with the left hand: The right hand supports the bell of the instrument. During the 1800s, the ancestors of the modern French horn did not have valves. The player changed the instrument's tone and pitch by inserting the right hand into the bell. While this technique is still used for some special effects, most French hornists now use the valves to change pitch.

The Tuba

As the largest brass instrument, the tuba has the lowest pitch. Tubas are available in several sizes. The most popular has about 18 feet of coiled-up tubing. The tubing is conical, like the French horn, giving the tuba a similarly deep, mellow tone quality.

Tubas are used in both bands and orchestras. They usually supply the lowest harmony parts, although they sometimes do carry the melody. The tuba part is particularly important in playing on the beats of highly rhythmic music.

The tuba rests on the player's lap. Despite its great size, the tuba does not require more breath to play than the smaller brass instruments. Even though the tuba can provide a powerful bass line, it can also be played lightly and daintily when necessary.

John Philip Sousa, the famous American bandmaster and composer of marches, invented a kind of tuba called the sousaphone. He based it on the helicon, a doughnut-shaped instrument like the *buccina*, that first appeared in 1875. The players put their bodies inside the circle of the sousaphone, resting it on one shoulder. The most striking feature of the sousaphone is the bell. It is a full 48 inches wide and can be turned to face in any direction. You frequently see the sousaphone in marching bands.

If the old Hebrew, Greek, Roman, or Viking trumpeters could step out of the history books, they would hardly recognize the offspring of the instruments they played so long ago. But they would soon realize that the basic principles have stayed the same over all these centuries. And with a little practice they surely could master any one of today's brass instruments.

Making a Record

Nowhere are science and music more closely combined than in the recording studio. The bond that joins them is electricity. Electricity carries the sounds of music to the finished recording—tape, record, or compact disc.

The Microphone

The first step in the recording process is to change musical sounds into patterns of electricity. This is the job of the microphone. (Microphones do not make sounds louder, as some people believe.)

Every sound, you recall, has two parts: frequency and amplitude.

The frequency, or speed of vibration, determines the pitch. The overtones that are added to the basic tone give the sound its particular tone quality.

The amplitude, or wideness of the vibrations, determines the loudness or softness of the tone.

Suppose you sing two notes into a microphone. The first has a frequency of 800 vibrations per second. The microphone sends out 800 tiny bursts of electrical current every second. The second note, which is lower, vibrates 300 times a second. For this note, the microphone sends out only 300 electrical bursts per second.

Let's say you sing two more notes into a microphone. These notes each have a frequency of 600. But the first note is much louder than the second one. Although the microphone sends out 600 bursts of electricity for each note, there is more electricity in every burst of the loud note.

In this way the microphone converts the frequency and amplitude of the live sounds into a flow of electricity. And the pattern of electricity has the same frequency and amplitude as the original sound.

The flow of electricity in a microphone can be compared to bullets shot from an imaginary machine gun—a gun that can shoot bullets of any size at any speed. When the microphone picks up tones of high frequency, it sends out hundreds or thousands of bursts of electricity per second. That is like the machine gun firing bullets very rapidly. For notes of low frequency, fewer bursts come out in the same time. That is like the machine gun firing its bullets more slowly.

When the tones are loud (the amplitude is wide), the microphone sends out stronger bursts of electricity. This can be compared to the firing of bigger bullets. If the tone is soft, there is less electricity in each burst. That is like shooting smaller bullets.

The most popular kind of microphone used in recording studios is probably the dynamic, or moving coil, microphone. The front consists of a very thin, flexible metal plate, called the diaphragm. Attached to the back of the diaphragm is a coil of very fine wire. The coil is placed so that it can move freely between the poles of a permanent magnet.

The sound waves strike the diaphragm and set it vibrating. This moves the coil rapidly back and forth near the magnet. Each movement creates a tiny electrical current in the coil. The pitch determines the speed of vibrations of the diaphragm and the frequency of the little pulses of electricity. The loudness determines the wideness of the diaphragm vibrations and the strength of each electrical pulse. In this way, the microphone changes the mechanical vibrations of the original sound wave into an identical electrical pattern.

Recording engineers consider the dynamic microphone an excellent all-purpose microphone. It is sturdy, picks up most frequencies equally, and is not too expensive. The main drawback is its inability to pick up very high or very low frequencies.

· 117 ·

Another favorite of professionals is the condenser, or capacitor, microphone. The heart of the condenser microphone is a metal diaphragm that is set parallel to a fixed

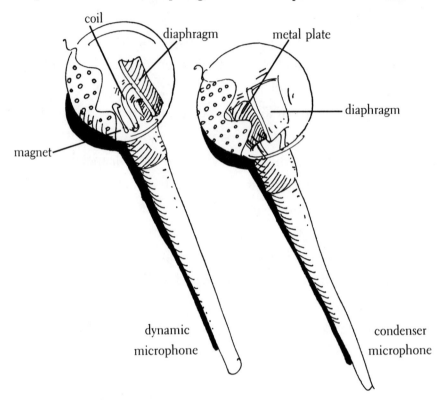

coil
diaphragm
metal plate
magnet
diaphragm
dynamic
microphone
condenser
microphone

metal plate. An outside electrical current is fed to the diaphragm and the plate. When sound waves strike this microphone, the diaphragm vibrates back and forth. It moves toward and away from the fixed plate.

Each time the diaphragm moves toward the plate, a tiny spurt of electricity flows in the circuit. The frequency of the spurts depends on the frequency of the original sound.

If the sound is loud, the diaphragm moves closer to the plate and there is a big flow of electricity. With softer sounds, less electricity flows in each spurt.

The condenser microphone is a superb recording instrument. But it can be difficult to use. It is an excellent choice for recording the human voice, as well as woodwind, brass, and percussion instruments. It is not as good for recording the strings. Good-quality condenser microphones are very expensive and can be easily damaged by rough handling.

Microphone Specifications

Both dynamic and condenser microphones are available in many different models and a range of prices. How do you tell which is best for which purpose?

The specifications, or "specs," that come with each microphone list its technical features. Among the most important specs are polar pattern, frequency response, impedance, and sensitivity.

Polar pattern refers to the way the microphone "hears." Some microphones receive sounds only from the front. Others pick up sounds from all directions. And still others accept sounds from the front and back only.

The most popular polar pattern hears only, or mostly, the sounds that arrive from in front. Because its hearing area is heart (cardiac) shaped, it is known as cardioid pattern.

Sound engineers use cardioid microphones to record orchestras or bands in a studio. They aim the microphones at the instruments or sections they want to pick up. These microphones are also used to record performers live in concert halls or night clubs. The chief advantage here is that they keep out audience noise. And they are preferred for recording the sounds of speech. In addition to their other benefits, cardioid microphones cut out echoes and reverberations.

To create a feeling of space and reverberation, engineers often work with the omnidirectional microphone. This kind of microphone does more than pick up sound from the music source. It also collects all the sounds reflected from the walls and ceiling, giving the effect of listening in a large room. Omnidirectional microphones are often chosen to record performers who sing and accompany themselves on the guitar. Using two such mikes, one for the voice and one for the guitar, makes for a full and well-blended tone.

The bidirectional, or figure-8, microphone has more limited use than the others. It hears sounds that are directly in front and directly in back. Radio studios use these microphones in situations where two people are talking across a table to each other. And the bidirectional mike is best for duets and also for vocalists who want to face their accompaniment while they are singing.

The frequency response spec gives the range of frequencies, or pitches, that the microphone can pick up. This spec

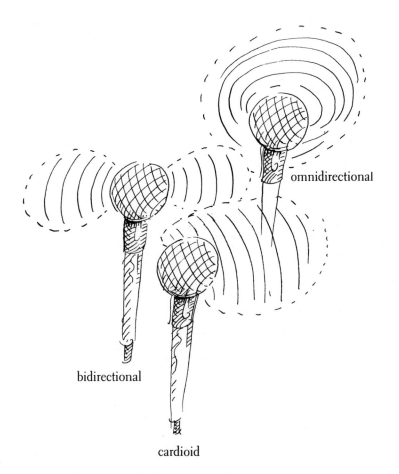

omnidirectional

bidirectional

cardioid

is sometimes called bandwidth. The human ear, you recall, can hear frequencies from about 20 to 20,000 vibrations per second. The very best microphones have a far wider range, from perhaps 5 to 40,000 vibrations per second. This extended range, even though it is not audible to us, contributes to the quality of the tone.

The minimum bandwidth for quality recording microphones is about 50 to 15,000 vibrations per second. The least expensive microphones only go from about 100 to 10,000. While cheap microphones record speech satisfactorily, they don't give very good results with music.

Impedance is a measure of resistance to the flow of electricity. Expressed in ohms, this figure tells how much the circuit inside the microphone blocks, or impedes, the electricity. For most purposes it is enough to know whether the microphone has high impedance (over 600 ohms) or low impedance (under 600 ohms).

Most tape recorders work best with low-impedance microphones. But these microphones sometimes pick up a hum from nearby electrical cables. When the cables connecting the microphone and tape recorder are over 15 feet long, a high-impedance microphone is preferred. This microphone, though, tends to lose the high-frequency pitches.

There is no ideal impedance for all situations. Generally, a microphone that matches the requirements of your tape recorder specs and avoids problems with hum or long microphone cables is best.

Sensitivity measures the intensity of a microphone signal in response to a sound wave of a certain strength. Unfortunately, this is a difficult feature to measure. Most microphone manufacturers indicate sensitivity as a negative figure in decibels, or dB. The higher the figure, the better. Thus, a microphone rated -50 dB is better than one rated -70 dB. A sensitivity of -55 dB is generally considered the lowest limit for quality recording. But even that is not essential. If your microphone is less sensitive, you can make up for it by turning up the tape recorder volume a little.

The Amplifier

When microphones change sound into patterns of electricity, they send out only tiny amounts of current. Before this small current can be used in the next step of the recording process, it must be built up, or amplified. This is done with an amplifier.

Amplifying the current is like making an enlargement of a photograph. The pattern of the current (like the photographic image) stays the same. But the entire flow of electricity (like the picture) is made larger.

Most home tape recorders have the amplifier built into the tape recorder itself. But in professional recording studios the amplifier is a separate unit. In both cases the highly complex electronic circuit within the amplifier makes the current up to 50,000 times stronger.

The Tape Recorder

In the recording process, the built-up current passes from the amplifier to a tape recorder. The tape recorder changes the patterns of electrical current into magnetic patterns on a recording tape.

The tapes used for recording are made of thin plastic bases coated with metal oxide. The metal oxide coating consists of immense numbers of tiny magnetic particles. They are only about a millionth of an inch long, but each one has a north and a south pole. On a new, blank tape these microscopic magnets are scattered along the tape facing in all directions.

All tapes are basically the same, but they come in different sizes and packages. They can be $\frac{1}{4}$ inch, $\frac{1}{2}$ inch, 1 inch, or 2 inches wide. Narrow ($\frac{1}{4}$ inch) tape is used for most home recording. The wider tapes, which can carry as many as sixteen separate tracks of sound, are found in professional recording studios. Professionals have to thread their tapes from one reel to another. Much of the tape for home use is packaged in self-contained cassettes.

Once the tape is loaded on the tape recorder, it moves past three heads. Each head is basically a ring of metal with a tiny gap in the ring. It is wrapped with a fine wire coil. When electricity flows through the wire coil, the metal ring becomes an electromagnet, with a very strong magnetic field at the gap.

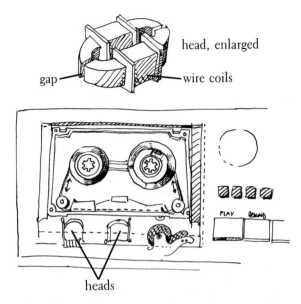

gap — head, enlarged — wire coils

heads

The three heads are known as the erase, record, and playback heads. (On most cassette recorders, there are only two heads; the record and playback heads are combined into one.)

Before recording, you want to be sure that the tape is blank. On a blank tape, the magnetized particles are not organized into any pattern. All new tape is blank. If you have a used tape, the old pattern must be erased. Erasing the tape involves feeding a high-frequency alternating current—switching rapidly from positive to negative and back—to erase the head. As the tape is drawn past this head, the alternating current jumbles and scatters the magnetized particles. This destroys any pattern they might have had and will improve the quality of the new recording.

The electrical signal from the microphone and amplifier

is fed to the coil in the record head. As the tape passes the gap in this head, the electrical current arranges the metal particles on the tape magnetically. The magnetic pattern copies the pattern of the electricity that comes from the amplifier.

The playback head allows you to hear what has been recorded. It works in reverse compared to the record head. In the record head, current in the coil magnetizes the tape. In the playback head, the magnetized particles on the tape create a current in the coil. This current is then used to reproduce the sounds of the original input.

Some wide tapes allow you to make multitrack recordings. These tapes have room for as many as sixteen separate channels, each one with its own instruments or voices.

Suppose you want to make a four-track tape of a rock group with a vocalist. You record the percussion on one track, the lead guitar on the second, the bass guitar on the third, and the vocalist on the fourth. Once you've got all four tracks recorded, you can listen to each track by itself or in combination with the others. Then you use an electronic device called a mixer to combine the individual tracks and create the one finished tape.

Tape recording also lets you correct mistakes. A performer rarely plays or sings perfectly on the first "take." Five, ten, or fifty takes may be needed before the artist, producer, and engineer agree that they have captured the best possible performance.

The tapes of a recording session may fill one or more large reels of tape. The tape editor goes through all the reels. He or she selects the best sections and splices, or joins, them together to make a single master tape. Splicing is an important part of almost every recording. When it is done well the entire piece sounds as though it was recorded in a single take. A good tape editor can even snip out a single wrong note and put in the right one!

Stereo Sound

From your seat in a concert hall, part of what you hear comes from the stage. The rest of the sound bounces off the walls and ceiling of the hall before it reaches your ears. Since the sounds come at you from all directions, they reach your ears at different times. For example, the sounds of the violins, seated to your left, reach your left ear first, and the bass fiddles, on your right, reach your right ear first. But in addition, the sounds reflected off the right side of the hall reach your right ear before they reach your left. And the sounds bouncing off the left side come to that ear first. The slight difference and delay give you the feeling of hearing live music in a big space.

Recordings have always been made to sound as much like live performances as possible. At first, though, the sounds of the music were picked up by only one microphone, or one group of microphones. This method, called monophonic, reproduced the sound of the music, but without the feeling of hearing it in an auditorium.

A big advance came in the 1950s with stereophonic, or stereo, recordings. To make a stereo recording, the engineers place two microphones, or groups of microphones, one on the right and one on the left side of the performers. They record two separate signals—one from the right, one from the left. The signals go separately through the amplifier and tape recorder. On the finished disc or tape the two signals are combined on one track. On the disc, the two channels of sound are recorded as wiggles (the actual sound waves are reproduced) on the right and left sides of the record groove. The needle picks them up separately and feeds them into opposite speakers. There are two parallel sound tracks on the tape, played through two separate speakers. The result in both cases is a sense of being at a concert with sound reaching your ears from all sides. (The word stereophonic comes from the Greek *stereos*, meaning solid, and *phone*, meaning sound.)

The Dolby System

The Dolby noise-reduction system, the invention of the American scientist Dr. Ray Dolby, is another improvement in recording music. The system gets rid of annoying tape hiss. Tape hiss is a high-frequency noise that is produced within the tape recorder by the tape passing over the head. It is most often heard during soft passages in the music. During loud passages, the music hides or masks the hissing sound.

Using the Dolby system, loud passages of the music are recorded exactly as they are performed. But the sound of the soft passages is boosted, or made louder, with a special lift given to the high-frequency tones.

The tape is then played back on a machine equipped with the Dolby system. The loud passages are played as recorded. But the soft sounds are reduced, since they were given an extra boost in the making of the recording. Tape hiss has a high frequency; so, with the soft tones, and especially the high-frequency tones, cut, the hiss is also reduced. The result is a virtually noise-free tape recording. Playing Dolbyized tape on equipment that lacks the Dolby system, however, gives you sound that is shrill and has too many high-pitched tones.

Manufacture

The manufacture of the recordings—discs or tapes—begins with the master tape. The next step in disc manufacture is to cut a master disc from a blank made of aluminum coated with a mirror-smooth layer of black, shiny lacquer.

A worker places the disc on the turntable of a machine called a cutting lathe. Above the turntable is the bridge. The bridge holds the sharp needle that will cut the groove in the disc. The spiral shape of the groove results from the

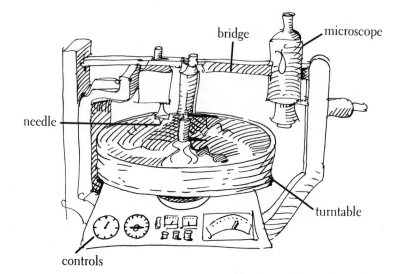

bridge

microscope

needle

turntable

controls

cutting needle slowly moving across the bridge while the record turns beneath it.

The master tape is then played into the cutting lathe. The taped sound causes the cutting needle to vibrate from side to side. As the needle cuts the spiral groove, it is cutting the actual sound wave into the surface of the master disc.

When the entire groove is cut, a thin layer of metal is applied to the master disc and then removed. This metal layer, called a stamper, is a negative, or reverse, image of the original. The groove on the original is the raised spiral on the stamper. The raised part between the grooves on the original is a groove on the stamper. If many thousands of copies of the record are needed, several stampers have to be made from the original master disc.

The stampers, one for each side of the record, are placed in a record-making press. The record itself is made from a "biscuit" of vinyl, about half the size and twice as thick as the final record. The biscuit is warmed. When slightly soft it is placed in the press by the operator. Hot steam behind each stamper melts the plastic so that it flows easily into all the grooves.

After a few seconds, cold water replaces the hot steam and the vinyl hardens. The operator opens the press, removes the finished record, and is ready to make the next record.

Cassette tapes are made in a tape-duplicating machine. The duplicating machine is really a whole bank of tape recorders, all hooked together. A blank tape is inserted in each of the tape recorders. The master tape signal is fed to all of them at once, so that all the tapes are magnetized simultaneously.

At normal speed it can take up to an hour and a half to copy both sides of a cassette tape. To hasten the process, both the master tape and the blank tapes are played at a very high speed. As a result, both sides can be copied in little more than one minute!

Compact Discs

The latest advance in recording technology is the compact disc, or CD. The CD is a lot smaller than a standard record—4.75 inches versus 12 inches across. And it has a shiny metal (aluminum) surface instead of black vinyl. Most experts agree that CDs produce an especially clear sound. Compared to tapes and records, CDs can record a wider range of frequencies and of loudness without distortion. It also has none of the hiss, rumble, and surface noise of the conventional records or tapes.

Compact discs are essentially digital recordings, while the older-style records are analog recordings. Analog recordings store the sound as continuously changing frequencies and amplitudes, either in the form of a wiggly record groove or in the pattern of magnetic particles on the tape. Digital recordings, on the other hand, store the sound in the form of a long series of numbers that describe the sound waves.

A computer built into the CD recording equipment measures the frequency, amplitude, and tone quality of the sound 48,000 times a second. Each of those sound measurements is then described by a code number. It is a binary number, like all numbers used by computers. In the binary system just two symbols, 0 and 1, are used to express all the numbers. A group of sixteen 0's and/or 1's (each of which is called a bit) describes each sound measurement.

A master tape is made at the digital recording session, just as at the more traditional recording sessions. The CD master tape, though, is very different from the older kinds. Here, the particles are arranged to store a series of numbers instead of the sound waves. It is closer to the pattern of particles on a computer or video tape than to the pattern on the usual audio tape.

The master tape goes into the machine that makes a master disc. A laser beam inside the machine cuts a series of microscopic pits into the surface of a blank CD in response to the signal from the master tape.

The pits and flat spots on the disc correspond to the 0's and 1's of the binary code. For example, a particular note might be identified by the sixteen-bit code 1101 0101 1000 0110. That would be translated on the CD into "pit-pit-flat-pit; flat-pit-flat-pit; pit-flat-flat-flat; flat-pit-pit-flat."

The pits and flat spots are microscopic in size. They are about 0.4 microns wide and 0.2 microns deep. To give you an idea of how tiny they are, the period at the end of this sentence is about 500 microns in diameter. The pits and flats are also packed tightly together. There are 85,000 of them to an inch. And they are arranged in a spiral—starting at the center and moving out to the edge—that is three miles long. All together there are around six billion bits of information on the disc. With this tight fit, about an hour and a quarter's worth of music can be squeezed onto a single side of a CD. The other side is left blank for the label.

Workers then make a mold from the original master disc. Using the mold in a presser, they produce as many plastic copies as are needed. The plastic is then coated with a thin layer of aluminum. Finally, the CD is sealed with a protective layer of clear plastic.

Making recordings—disc, tape, or CD—is the perfect wedding of science and music. But a recording by itself is a silent piece of plastic or metal. To be turned into sound, the recording must be played back—which is the subject of our next chapter.

Playback

You keep books on the shelf so that you can read them whenever you want. All you need to do is open a book and start turning the pages. In the same way, you store music on records so that you can play them back at will. But there is a difference. To hear the sound of music, you must have some sort of playback equipment—a record player, tape recorder, or CD player—that will produce sound waves you can hear.

The Record Player

To play back a disc, or record, you need a record player. This piece of equipment was traditionally called a phonograph (or a gramophone in England), but today we usually call it a stereo. You place the record on the round, flat platform, or turntable, of the record player. The turntable revolves, or spins, carrying the record around and around. Classical and pop album records spin at 33⅓ revolutions per minute (rpm); pop singles at 45 or 33⅓ rpm. Some turntables also spin at 78 rpm (for records made before the mid-1950s) and at 16⅔ rpm (for "talking book" records).

The turntable's spin must be absolutely steady—never speeding up or slowing down. Any variation will change the pitch of the sound. Wow, flutter, and rumble are names given to the sound distortions that can result from poor turntables. On good turntables, the wow and flutter should be no more than 0.1%. The rumble rating, or signal-to-noise ratio (S/N), should be at least −45 dB.

Every turntable is built around an electric motor. One basic kind is the induction motor. While it is inexpensive, this motor does not always spin the turntable at a steady speed. Another type is the more costly synchronous motor, which spins the turntable very evenly. And the most expensive are the servo motors, motors that continuously measure the speed of rotation and make immediate adjustments as necessary.

There are three possible ways to connect the electric motor to the turntable. In the belt drive, a rubber or plastic belt runs from the motor to the turntable. In the rim drive, the motor turns a rubber wheel that spins the turntable by

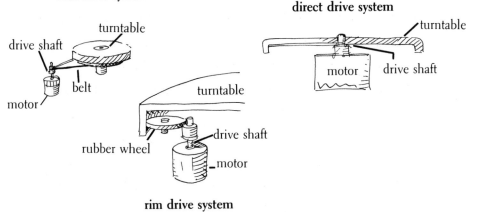

belt drive system

turntable

drive shaft

belt

motor

turntable

drive shaft

motor

rubber wheel

rim drive system

direct drive system

turntable

motor   drive shaft

pressing against the inside rim of the turntable from below. And in the direct drive, the motor is connected right to the turntable, without a belt or wheel. Usually, direct drive produces the best sound.

Some turntables have speed indicators and controls to adjust their speed. The speed indicator is usually a series of short up-and-down lines printed on the side of the record platter. The lines are lit by a stroboscopic light, one that flashes on and off at a fixed rate. If the lines appear to be standing still, the turntable is spinning at the correct speed. If the lines are moving forward, the turntable is spinning too fast. And if they are moving backward, the turntable is too slow.

Located to the side of the turntable is the tone arm, a

long, thin, metal beam, bearing electric wiring, that swings out over the turntable. At the tip of the tone arm is the cartridge. And inside the cartridge is the stylus, a tiny chip of diamond or sapphire. The stylus is the only part of the pickup that actually touches the grooves of the record.

As the record spins on the turntable, the stylus vibrates back and forth along the wiggly record groove. The two main stylus specs are tracking force and compliance. Tracking force is the smallest downward force necessary to keep the stylus in the groove without hopping around. It should be as low as possible, since the greater the force, the greater the wear on both stylus and record. Tracking force is usually expressed in grams and should be between 2.5 and 4 grams.

Compliance shows how well the stylus is able to follow the curves of the record groove. The higher the compliance figure, the better. The spec usually indicates how far the stylus bends (in centimeters) per unit of force (in dynes). A compliance figure of at least 8×10^{-6} cm/dyne is desirable. A figure of, say, 7×10^{-6} cm/dyne would be too low.

The tiny cartridge works on the same scientific principle as the giant generators in electric power plants. A magnet moved near a coil of wire or a coil moved near a magnet generates an electric current in the wire of the coil.

In the moving-magnet cartridge, the magnet is attached to the shank that holds the stylus. As the stylus vibrates through the record groove, it passes the vibrations on to the magnet. The magnet swings between two coils of wire—

one for the left stereo signal, one for the right. This creates an electrical current in each coil that follows the pitch and loudness of the original sound.

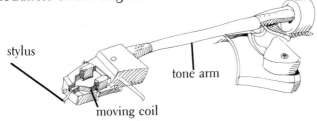

stylus

tone arm

moving coil

The moving-coil cartridge has two coils attached to the stylus. The coils vibrate within a magnetic field. This vibration creates a small electrical current that follows the changes of pitch and loudness of the original sound.

Perhaps the most important spec of a cartridge is its frequency response. This figure tells you the range of frequencies the cartridge can pick up. The lowest frequency response for high-quality sound is from 30 to 18,000 vibrations per second. The wider the range, the better the cartridge. It should also have a "flat" response—that is, it should reproduce all the frequencies and amplitudes evenly.

Tape Machines

Music recorded on tape cassettes or reel-to-reel tapes may be played back on a tape deck or tape recorder. Both of these machines work like the tape recorder used in making tape recordings.

Tape decks are part of most modern sound systems. The

deck moves, or transports, the tape past the three standard heads—erase, record, and playback (see pages 124–125). In standard machines, the tape moves past the heads at a speed of 7½ inches per second (ips). Some machines have slower tape speeds, of 3¾ or 1⅞ ips. Professional tape recordings are usually made at 15 ips. You can either make and listen to your own tape recordings or just play back tapes that have already been recorded. For you to hear the tapes, though, the tape deck must be hooked up to an amplifier and speaker—two speakers for stereo sound.

A tape recorder has the same three heads as the tape deck. But it also has a built-in amplifier and speaker. The tape recorder is not usually part of a sound system, but is a separate unit.

The Compact Disc Player

The compact disc, or *CD*, is flat and round like a regular phonograph record. But there the similarity ends. A record, as you know, has a spiral groove cut into the surface. A CD, on the other hand, contains a three-mile spiral track of tiny pits that represent the computer-style numbers required to reproduce exactly the recorded sounds.

The CD player changes this pattern of pits into sound differently from both a phonograph and a tape player. You slip the CD into the player, music side down. The mechanism starts spinning the disc at a speed of 500 revolutions per minute (rpm). Underneath the CD is a laser beam. The laser is focused to a point smaller than the width of a human hair.

Starting at the center of the disc and slowly moving out to the edge, the laser shines up at the track of pits. When the laser strikes a flat spot, it reflects the light back to a photo detector (light detector). When the laser strikes a pit, the pit does not reflect the light and no light reaches the photo detector.

The photo detector registers the arrangements of pits and flat spots as fast as they pass by on the spinning disc. It sends this information to a special electronic circuit, called a digital-to-analog converter. This circuit changes the coded information into the same electrical pattern as comes from a conventional record or a tape.

The reason there is no surface noise on a CD is that at no time in the recording or playback process does anything touch the surface of the CD to create friction, which makes noise.

The Amplifier

The record player, tape recorder, and CD player all give off electrical charges or currents that vary according to the pattern on the disc or tape being played. Although the sources are different, the electrical impulses are alike in one way—they are all very weak. Before the signals can be heard, they must be made stronger in an amplifier.

Most amplifiers, or amps, have two parts. The pream-plifier, or preamp, is where the weak signals receive their first boost. Some of the signals are so weak that they are measured in millivolts, or thousandths of a volt. In the preamp these signals are amplified up to at least one-half volt. A well-designed preamp amplifies all sounds equally—it does not favor some and cut back on others.

The preamp sends the signals with the higher voltage to the amplifier. The amp then raises the power of the signal. Signal power is measured in watts. The amp for a sound system should put out at least 10 watts of continuous power for each of the two stereo channels. An output of more than 80 watts of power is considered wasteful.

The Speaker System

The amplified electrical impulses are carried to the part of the playback system called the speakers or loudspeakers. The speakers change the electrical vibrations back into sound.

The speaker consists of a stiff paper cone. Attached to the cone is a coil of wire that is placed between the poles of a permanent magnet. When the varying electrical signal from the amplifier passes to the coil, it causes the coil to vibrate toward and away from the magnet. As the coil vibrates, it causes the cone to vibrate, sending sound waves out into the air.

Almost every playback system has a number of speakers. There must be at least two to provide for the two channels of stereo sound. And for good sound quality there should be separate speakers of different sizes to cover the full range of frequencies.

The large ones, named woofers, are between 7 and 15 inches across. They are good for producing the low-frequency sounds. Small speakers, called tweeters, are between 1 and 3 inches in diameter. They are considered best for the high frequencies. And speakers of medium size, termed midrange drivers, are about 4 inches across. The midrange drivers excel at picking up the middle frequencies.

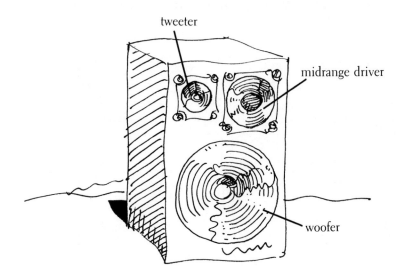

tweeter

midrange driver

woofer

Two, three, or four speakers are usually mounted together in a box, or enclosure. A so-called crossover network divides the electrical signals from the amp. The network sends each particular frequency to the speaker designed to handle it.

Stereo records and tapes are intended to be played through two or more sets of speakers, one set for each track of sound. When the speaker sets are at a distance from each other, the sound seems to come from a wide area, giving it a lifelike, three-dimensional quality.

The quality of the speaker's sound depends very much on how the speaker is mounted in the enclosure. The most popular mounting is the air suspension, also known as the acoustic suspension mounting. It is often used in small,

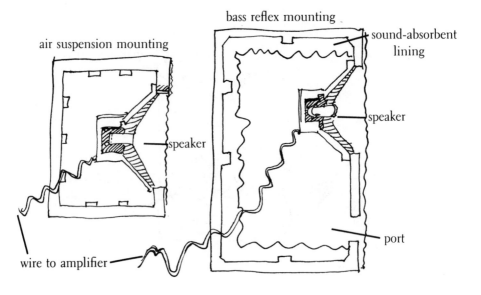

bookshelf-size speaker systems. The cone of the speaker is loosely mounted over a round hole cut in the front side of a sealed wooden box. The entire front is covered with a grille made of coarse cloth.

The bass reflex is another type of enclosure. Here the cone is rigidly mounted in a hole in a sealed box. The box is lined with thick, sound-absorbing material. Beneath the hole for the speaker is another opening, called a port. The port allows the vibrations produced by the rear of the cone to escape into the air. These vibrations reinforce the vibrations produced by the front of the cone—particularly the low frequencies—and improve the quality of the sound.

Speaker system specs often include information on frequency response (50 to 18,000 vibrations per second should be a minimum) and maximum power (at least 50 watts). But with the speakers, more than with any other part of the sound system, your ears are your best guide in deciding which is best.

It was many millennia ago that primitive scientific principles were applied to make the earliest musical instruments. And it was just over a hundred years ago that a new relationship between science and music was established to make possible the recording of sound. Since these beginnings amazing advances have been made. Yet the quest for better-sounding instruments and more natural-sounding recordings goes on.

Musicians are still asking scientists and instrument makers, "Is there a way you can give this instrument a more beautiful tone and make it easier to play?"

Music lovers are still asking the record companies, "Can you make records or tapes that sound more like the live sound in a concert hall?"

And scientists are still asking the public, "Do you think this new kind of instrument or this new piece of equipment improves the sound of music?"

For Further Reading

Benade, Arthur H. *Horns, Strings and Harmony.* Westport, CT: Greenwood Press, 1979.

Berger, Melvin. *The Photo Dictionary of the Orchestra.* New York: Methuen, 1980.

———. *The Stereo-Hi Fi Handbook.* New York: Lothrop, 1979.

———. *The Trumpet Book.* New York: Lothrop, 1978.

Camras, Marvin, ed. *Magnetic Tape Recording.* New York: Van Nostrand, 1985.

Crowhurst, Norman H. *Electronic Musical Instruments.* Blue Ridge Summit, PA: Tab, 1971.

Mackay, Andy. *Electronic Music.* London: Harrow House, 1981.

Marcuse, Sibyl. *A Survey of Musical Instruments*. New York: Harper, 1975,

Unger-Hamilton, Clive. *Keyboard Instruments*. Minneapolis, MN: Control Data Publishing, 1981.

Since the technology for sound recording and playback is changing so rapidly, the best sources of current information are such magazines as:

Audio
Digital Audio
High Fidelity
Stereo Review

Index

Numbers in *italics* refer to illustrations.

Adam's apple. *See* larynx
air suspension enclosure, 144–
    45, *144*
alto flute, 91, *91*
amplifier, 123, 141–42
amplitude, 5, *5*, 6, 115, 116

Bach, Johann Sebastian, 76
bass clarinet, 94–95, *94*
bass drum, 49
bass flute, 91, *91*
bassoon, 84, 85, *85*, 99–101
bass reflex enclosure, *144*, 145
bell lyra, 64
Bohm, Theobald, 90
bongos, *47*, 48
bow, 36, 39–40
brass (instruments), 102–14
brass (metal), 103
bridge, 35–36, *36*
buccina, 102, *103*, 114
bugle, 107

cartridge, 138
    frequency response, 139
    moving coil, 139
    moving magnet, 138–39
castanets, *47*, 47, 57–59
CD. *See* compact disc
celesta, 66
'cello, 29, *29*, 35–43
chimes, *47*, 48, 66

clarinet, 82, 84, 85, *85*, 88, 92–
    95
claves, 47, *47*, 61
clavichord, 68–70, *69*
cochlea, *17*, 18
compact disc, 132–34
    player, 140–41
compliance, 138
computer, 82
contrabassoon, 100, *101*
cornet, 111
Cristofori, Bartolomeo, 71
cross-fingering, 87, 96, 98
cutting lathe, 129–30, *130*
cymbals, *47*, 47, 52–54

decibel, 6, 123
digital recording, 132–33
Dolby system, 128–29
double bass, 29, *29*, 35–40, 41–
    43
drum, *47*, 47, 48–51
dulcimer, 68, *69*

ear, 16–18, *17*
eardrum. *See* tympanum
echoes, 12–13
electric organ, 78–79
electronic organ, 78–79
English horn, 98–99, *98*

falsetto, 26
flute, *12*, 82, 84, 85, *85*, 89–91

French horn, 103, *103*, 112–13
frequency, 7, 8, *8*, 115–16

glockenspiel, *47*, *48*, 63–64
gong. *See* tam-tam
Guarneri, Giuseppe, 41–42
guitar, 29, *29*, 43–45

Hammond organ, 78
harp, 29–35, *29*, *33*
harpsichord, *69*, 70, 71
helicon, 114
high-hat cymbal, 54
hydraulis, 67, *69*

jingles (tambourine), 51–52

kettledrums. *See* timpani
keyboard, 67, 68, 72, 77, 80
keyboard instruments, 67–83

larynx, 19–22, *20*
loudness, 4–6, *5*, 26–27
loudspeaker, 142–45, *144*

maracas, *47*, 59–60
marimba, *48*, 63
microphone, 115–23, *118*
  bandwidth, 122
  condenser, 118–19
  dynamic, 117
  frequency response, 120–22
  impedance, 122
  polar pattern, 119–20, *121*
  sensitivity, 123
  specifications, 119–23
midrange driver, 143, *143*
mouthpiece, 92, *92*, 104, 108
  112
mute, 105

oboe, 82, 84, 85, *85*, 97–99
organ, 67, 76–78
  stops, 78
overblowing, 88, 94, 98, 100
overtones, 9–12, 24–25, 107,
  107, 108, 109, 112

pedals, 73–74, 77
percussion instruments, 46–66
piano, 66, 67–74, *73*
piccolo, 90, *91*, 93
pick-up, 44, *44*
pipe organ. *See* organ
pipes of Pan, 86–87
pitch, 7–8, 22, 46–47, 56, 62,
  87, 88, 97–98, 104, 106
pizzicato, 40
playback, 135–46
psalterv 68, *69*
Pythagoras, 74

recorder (instrument), 91
recording, 115–34
  manufacture, 129–32
reed, 92, *92*, 93, 96, 97, 99
resonance, 13–15, 22–23, *24*,
  59, 68
reverberation, 13
ride cymbal, 54
rosin, 40

sackbut, *103*, 108
salpinx, 102, *103*
santir, 68, *69*
Sax, Adolphe, 95
saxophone, 12, 85, *85*, 95–96,
  95
scale, tempered, 74–76
shofar, 102, *103*
sizzle cymbal, 54

snare drum, 48–49, *48*
snares, 48–49, *48*
sound waves, 2–3, 12, 16–17, 47, 82, 106
Sousa, John Philip, 114
sousaphone, 114
speaker, 142–45, *144*
Stradivari, Antonio, 41–43
stereo player, 135–39
stereophonic sound, 127–28
string instruments, 28–45
stylus, 138, *139*
synthesizer, 80–83, *80*

tambourine, 47, *47*, 51–52
tam-tam, 47, *47*, 54–56
tape recorder (tape deck), 124–27, *125*, 139–40
temple blocks, 47, *47*, 59
timpani, 47, 48, 61–62
tom-tom, 47, 48, 49, 55
tone arm, 137–38, *139*
tone quality, 9–12
tracking force, 138

triangle, 47, *47*, 56
trombone, 103, *103*, 108–9
trumpet, *12*, 103, *103*, 109–11
tuba, 103, *103*, 113–14
tubular bells. *See* chimes
turntable, 136–38, *137*
tweeter, 143, *143*
tympanum, 17, *17*

valve, 108, 109–11, *110*, 112
vibraphone, 47, 48, 64
viola, 29, *29*, 35–40, 41–43
violin, *12*, 29, *29*, 35–40, *36*, 41–43
vocal cords, 19–27, *20*
voice, 19–27

wood block, 47, *47*, 59
woodwind instruments, 84–101
woofer, 143, *143*

xylophone, 47, 48, 63, 64–66

zither, 68